NINJA Electric BBQ Grill & Smoker Cookbo

UK 2023

1500 Days of Healthy and Delicious

Ninja Wood Fire Electric Pellet Smoker Recipes

Misty L. Button

Warning-Disclaimer:

The purpose of this book is to educate and entertain. The author or publisher does not guarantee that anyone following the techniques, suggestions, tips, ideas, or strategies will become successful. The author and publisher shall have neither liability or responsibility to anyone with respect to any loss or damage caused, or alleged to be caused, directly or indirectly by the information contained in this book.

CONTENTS

Breakfastst Recipes 8

Cinnamon Sugar Roll-ups 8

Nut And Seed Muffins 8

Cream Cheese–stuffed French Toast 9

Bacon And Broccoli Bread Pudding 9

Spinach With Scrambled Eggs 10

Cinnamon Toast With Strawberries 10

Ham And Cheese Cups 11

Tomato-corn Frittata With Avocado Dressing 11

Cornflakes Toast Sticks 12

Banana And Oat Bread Pudding 12

Maple Walnut Pancake 13

Chocolate Banana Bread With White Chocolate 13

Crustless Broccoli Quiche 14

Grilled Sausage Mix 14

Egg And Avocado Burrito 15

Stuffed Bell Peppers With Italian Maple-glazed Sausage 15

Breakfast Chilaquiles 16

Ham And Corn Muffins 16

Honey-lime Glazed Grilled Fruit Salad 16

Mixed Berry Dutch Baby Pancake 17

Blueberry Dump Cake 17

Mini Caprese Pizzas 17

Chicken Breakfast Sausages 18

Fluffy Pancake Sheet 18

Sourdough Croutons 18

Avocado Quesadillas 19

Asparagus And Cheese Strata 19

Banana Bread 20

Mushroom And Squash Toast 20

Country-fried Steak And Eggs 21

Pesto Egg Croissantwiches 21

Cheesy Breakfast Casserole 22

Bacon And Egg Bread Cups 22

Meatless Recipes 23

Italian Baked Tofu 23

Eggplant Parmigiana 23

Spicy Cauliflower Roast 24

Honey-sriracha Brussels Sprouts 24

Grilled Mozzarella Eggplant Stacks 25

Broccoli And Tofu Teriyaki 25

Cheese And Spinach Stuffed Portobellos 26

Grilled Mozzarella And Tomatoes 26

Rosemary Roasted Potatoes 26

Perfect Grilled Asparagus 27

Loaded Zucchini Boats 27
Rosemary Roasted Squash With Cheese 27
Cheesy Asparagus And Potato Platter 28
Fast And Easy Asparagus 28
Buttered Broccoli With Parmesan 28
Cauliflower Steaks With Ranch Dressing 29
Cheesy Macaroni Balls 29
Corn Pakodas 30
Balsamic Mushroom Sliders With Pesto 30
Roasted Lemony Broccoli 30
Mozzarella Broccoli Calzones 31
Cheesy Broccoli Gratin 31
Veggie Taco Pie 32
Sriracha Golden Cauliflower 32
Simple Pesto Gnocchi 33
Grilled Artichokes With Garlic Aioli 33
Vegetarian Meatballs 34
Sweet Pepper Poppers 34
Vegetable And Cheese Stuffed Tomatoes 35
Sesame-thyme Whole Maitake Mushrooms 35
Crusted Brussels Sprouts With Sage 35
Beef Stuffed Bell Peppers 36
Grilled Vegetable Quesadillas 36

Sides, Snacks & Appetizers Recipes 37
Cheesy Apple Roll-ups 37
Avocado Egg Rolls 37
Cayenne Sesame Nut Mix 38
Maple Butter Corn Bread 38
Breaded Green Olives 39
Goat Cheese Bruschetta With Tomatoes 39
Homemade Bbq Chicken Pizza 39
Cheesy Steak Fries 40
French Fries 40
Sweet Potato Chips 40
Mushroom And Spinach Calzones 41
Balsamic Broccoli 41
Crispy Spiced Potatoes 42
Spicy Kale Chips 42
Crispy Cod Fingers 42
Easy Muffuletta Sliders With Olives 43
One-pot Nachos 43
Jalapeño Poppers 44
Brussels Sprouts And Bacon 44
Mozzarella Sticks 44
Cheese And Ham Stuffed Baby Bella 45
Buttermilk Marinated Chicken Wings 45
Cheesy Garlic Bread 46
Sweet Potato Fries With Honey-butter Sauce 46

Grilled Carrots With Honey Glazed 47

Sauces, Dips, And Dressings Recipes **47**
Lemon Dijon Vinaigrette 47
Garlic Lime Tahini Dressing 47
Balsamic Dressing 48
Pico De Gallo 48

Meats Recipes **48**
Pork Spareribs With Peanut Sauce 48
Pork Sausage With Cauliflower Mash 49
Cheesy Jalapeño Popper Burgers 49
Potato And Prosciutto Salad 50
Crispy Pork Tenderloin 50
Easy Beef Schnitzel 50
Apple-glazed Pork 51
Pork Chops In Bourbon 51
Tomato And Lamb Stew 52
Spicy Beef Lettuce Wraps 52
Vietnamese Pork Chops 53
Rosemary And Garlic Lamb Pitas 53
Mozzarella Meatball Sandwiches With Basil 54
Pulled Pork Sandwiches 54
Bacon Burger Meatballs 55
Bacon-wrapped Sausage With Tomato Relish 55
Korean-style Steak Tips 56
Lamb Rack With Pistachio 56
Sweet And Tangy Beef 57
Green Curry Beef 57
Teriyaki Pork And Mushroom Rolls 58
Sizzling Pork Sisig 58
Balsamic Honey Mustard Lamb Chops 59
Crackling Pork Roast 59
Rack Of Lamb Chops With Rosemary 59
Fast Lamb Satay 60
Beef And Vegetable Cubes 60
Baby Back Ribs In Gochujang Marinade 61
Spaghetti Squash Lasagna 61
Uncle's Famous Tri-tip 62
Swedish Beef Meatballs 62
Steak And Lettuce Salad 63
Pork Chops With Creamy Mushroom Sauce 63
Carne Asada Tacos 64
Smoky Paprika Pork And Vegetable Kabobs 64

Poultry Recipes **65**
Pecan-crusted Turkey Cutlets 65
Roasted Chicken Tenders With Veggies 65
Grilled Cornish Hens 66
Lemony Chicken And Veggie Kebabs 66

Sweet Chili Turkey Kebabs 67
Salsa Verde Chicken Enchiladas 67
Stuffed Spinach Chicken Breast 68
Easy Asian Turkey Meatballs 68
Teriyaki Chicken And Bell Pepper Kebabs 69
Buttermilk Ranch Chicken Tenders 69
Dill Chicken Strips 70
Glazed Duck With Cherry Sauce 70
Garlic Brown-butter Chicken With Tomatoes 71
Lime-garlic Grilled Chicken 71
Maple-teriyaki Chicken Wings 72
Orange And Honey Glazed Duck With Apples 72
Turkey Meatballs With Cranberry Sauce 73
Crispy Chicken Strips 73
Herbed Grilled Chicken Thighs 74
Spicy Chicken Kebabs 74
Spiced Breaded Chicken Cutlets 75
Honey Rosemary Chicken 75
Simple Whole Chicken Bake 75
Fried Chicken Piccata 76
Lemon And Rosemary Chicken 76

Seafood Recipes 77
Tomato-stuffed Grilled Sole 77
Orange-ginger Soy Salmon 77
Shrimp Boil 78
Honey-walnut Shrimp 78
Mom's Lemon-pepper Salmon 79
Coconut Shrimp With Orange Chili Sauce 79
Chili-lime Shrimp Skewers 80
Lemon-garlic Butter Scallops 80

Desserts Recipes 81
Blackberry Chocolate Cake 81
Simple Corn Biscuits 81
Chia Pudding 82
Pear And Apple Crisp 82
Classic Pound Cake 82
Grilled Apple Fries With Caramel Cream Cheese Dip 83
Orange Cake 83
Grilled Strawberry Pound Cake 84
Coffee Chocolate Cake 84
Chocolate And Peanut Butter Lava Cupcakes 85
Strawberry Pizza 85
Chocolate S'mores 86
Chocolate Pecan Pie 86
Easy Blackberry Cobbler 86
Grilled Banana S'mores 87
Everyday Cheesecake 87

Candied Pecans 88

Peaches-and-cake Skewers 88

Fudge Pie 89

Churros With Chocolate-yogurt Sauce 89

Peanut Butter-chocolate Bread Pudding 90

Curry Peaches, Pears, And Plums 90

Rum Grilled Pineapple Sundaes 91

Ultimate Skillet Brownies 91

Cinnamon-sugar Dessert Chips 92

Black And White Brownies 92

RECIPES INDEX **93**

Breakfastst Recipes

Cinnamon Sugar Roll-ups

Servings: 4
Cooking Time: 10 Minutes
Ingredients:

- 1 sheet frozen puff pastry, thawed
- 3 tablespoons cinnamon
- 5 tablespoons granulated sugar
- 2 tablespoons unsalted butter, melted, divided

Directions:

1. Insert the Grill Grate and close the hood. Select GRILL, set the temperature to LO, and set the time to 10 minutes. Select START/STOP to begin preheating.
2. While the unit is preheating, unroll the pastry dough on a flat surface. In a small bowl, combine the cinnamon and the sugar. Brush 1 tablespoon of butter over the surface of the pastry. Then sprinkle on the cinnamon sugar evenly.
3. Carefully roll the pastry into a log. Using a sharp knife, cut the log into 1- to 2-inch slices. Lightly brush the top and bottom of the roll-ups with the remaining 1 tablespoon of butter.
4. When the unit beeps to signify it has preheated, place the roll-ups on the Grill Grate. Close the hood and grill for 5 minutes.
5. After 5 minutes, open the hood and flip the roll-ups. Close the hood and cook for 5 minutes more.
6. When cooking is complete, the roll-ups will be a nice golden brown. Serve.

Nut And Seed Muffins

Servings:8
Cooking Time: 10 Minutes
Ingredients:

- ½ cup whole-wheat flour, plus 2 tablespoons
- ¼ cup oat bran
- 2 tablespoons flaxseed meal
- ¼ cup brown sugar
- ½ teaspoon baking soda
- ½ teaspoon baking powder
- ¼ teaspoon salt
- ½ teaspoon cinnamon
- ½ cup buttermilk
- 2 tablespoons melted butter
- 1 egg
- ½ teaspoon pure vanilla extract
- ½ cup grated carrots
- ¼ cup chopped pecans
- ¼ cup chopped walnuts
- 1 tablespoon pumpkin seeds
- 1 tablespoon sunflower seeds
- Cooking spray

Directions:

1. Select BAKE, set the temperature to 330ºF, and set the time to 10 minutes. Select START/STOP to begin preheating.
2. In a large bowl, stir together the flour, bran, flaxseed meal, sugar, baking soda, baking powder, salt, and cinnamon.
3. In a medium bowl, beat together the buttermilk, butter, egg, and vanilla. Pour into flour mixture and stir just until dry ingredients moisten. Do not beat.
4. Gently stir in carrots, nuts, and seeds.
5. Double up the foil cups so you have 8 total and spritz with cooking spray.
6. Put 4 foil cups in the pot and divide half the batter among them.
7. Close the hood and BAKE for 10 minutes, or until a toothpick inserted in center comes out clean.
8. Repeat step 7 to bake remaining 4 muffins.
9. Serve warm.

Cream Cheese–stuffed French Toast

Servings: 6
Cooking Time: 6 Minutes
Ingredients:

- 2 large eggs
- 1 cup milk
- 1 teaspoon cinnamon
- 1 teaspoon light brown sugar, packed
- 1 teaspoon vanilla extract
- 1 (8-ounce) package whipped cream cheese (flavored or plain)
- 12 slices white bread

Directions:

1. Insert the Grill Grate and close the hood. Select GRILL, set the temperature to HI, and set the time to 6 minutes. Select START/STOP to begin preheating.
2. While the unit is preheating, in a small bowl, whisk together the eggs, milk, cinnamon, brown sugar, and vanilla.
3. Spread a thick layer of cream cheese on one side of 6 bread slices. Top each with the remaining 6 bread slices. Dip the sandwich into the egg mixture, making sure to coat both sides completely.
4. When the unit beeps to signify it has preheated, place the French toast sandwiches on the Grill Grate. Close the hood and grill for 3 minutes.
5. After 3 minutes, open the hood and flip the French toast. Close the hood and continue cooking for 3 minutes more.
6. When cooking is complete, remove the French toast from the grill and serve.

Bacon And Broccoli Bread Pudding

Servings: 2 To 4
Cooking Time: 48 Minutes
Ingredients:

- ½ pound thick cut bacon, cut into ¼-inch pieces
- 3 cups brioche bread, cut into ½-inch cubes
- 2 tablespoons butter, melted
- 3 eggs
- 1 cup milk
- ½ teaspoon salt
- Freshly ground black pepper, to taste
- 1 cup frozen broccoli florets, thawed and chopped
- 1½ cups grated Swiss cheese

Directions:

1. Insert the Crisper Basket and close the hood. Select AIR CRISP, set the temperature to 400ºF, and set the time to 10 minutes. Select START/STOP to begin preheating.
2. Put the bacon in the basket. Close the hood and AIR CRISP for 8 minutes until crispy, shaking the basket a few times to help it cook evenly. Remove the bacon and set it aside on a paper towel.
3. AIR CRISP the brioche bread cubes for 2 minutes to dry and toast lightly.
4. Butter a cake pan. Combine all the remaining ingredients in a large bowl and toss well. Transfer the mixture to the buttered cake pan, cover with aluminum foil and refrigerate the bread pudding overnight, or for at least 8 hours.
5. Remove the cake pan from the refrigerator an hour before you plan to bake and let it sit on the countertop to come to room temperature.
6. Select BAKE, set the temperature to 330ºF, and set the time to 40 minutes. Select START/STOP to begin preheating.
7. Place the covered cake pan directly in the pot. Fold the ends of the aluminum foil over the top of the pan. Close the hood and BAKE for 20 minutes. Remove the foil and bake for an additional 20 minutes. If the top browns a little too much before the custard has set, simply return the foil to the pan. The bread pudding has cooked through when a skewer inserted into the center comes out clean.
8. Serve warm.

Spinach With Scrambled Eggs

Servings: 2

Cooking Time: 10 Minutes

Ingredients:

- 2 tablespoons olive oil
- 4 eggs, whisked
- 5 ounces fresh spinach, chopped
- 1 medium tomato, chopped
- 1 teaspoon fresh lemon juice
- ½ teaspoon coarse salt
- ½ teaspoon ground black pepper
- ½ cup of fresh basil, roughly chopped

Directions:

1. Grease a baking pan with the oil, tilting it to spread the oil around.

2. Select BAKE, set the temperature to 280°F, and set the time to 10 minutes. Select START/STOP to begin preheating.

3. In the pan, mix the remaining ingredients, apart from the basil leaves, whisking well until everything is completely combined.

4. Place the pan directly in the pot. Close the hood and BAKE for 10 minutes.

5. Top with fresh basil leaves before serving.

Cinnamon Toast With Strawberries

Servings: 4

Cooking Time: 10 Minutes

Ingredients:

- 1 can full-fat coconut milk, refrigerated overnight
- ½ tablespoon powdered sugar
- 1½ teaspoons vanilla extract, divided
- 1 cup halved strawberries
- 1 tablespoon maple syrup, plus more for garnish
- 1 tablespoon brown sugar, divided
- ¾ cup lite coconut milk
- 2 large eggs
- ½ teaspoon ground cinnamon
- 2 tablespoons unsalted butter, at room temperature
- 4 slices challah bread

Directions:

1. Turn the chilled can of full-fat coconut milk upside down (do not shake the can), open the bottom, and pour out the liquid coconut water. Scoop the remaining solid coconut cream into a medium bowl. Using an electric hand mixer, whip the cream for 3 to 5 minutes, until soft peaks form.

2. Add the powdered sugar and ½ teaspoon of the vanilla to the coconut cream, and whip it again until creamy. Place the bowl in the refrigerator.

3. Insert the Grill Grate and close the hood. Select GRILL, set the temperature to MAX, and set the time to 15 minutes. Select START/STOP to begin preheating.

4. While the unit is preheating, combine the strawberries with the maple syrup and toss to coat evenly. Sprinkle evenly with ½ tablespoon of the brown sugar.

5. In a large shallow bowl, whisk together the lite coconut milk, eggs, the remaining 1 teaspoon of vanilla, and cinnamon.

6. When the unit beeps to signify it has preheated, place the strawberries on the Grill Grate. Gently press the fruit down to maximize grill marks. Close the hood and GRILL for 4 minutes without flipping.

7. Meanwhile, butter each slice of bread on both sides. Place one slice in the egg mixture and let it soak for 1 minute. Flip the slice over and soak it for another minute. Repeat with the remaining bread slices. Sprinkle each side of the toast with the remaining ½ tablespoon of brown sugar.

8. After 4 minutes, remove the strawberries from the grill and set aside. Decrease the temperature to HIGH. Place the bread on the Grill Grate; close the hood and GRILL for 4 to 6 minutes until golden and caramelized. Check often to ensure desired doneness.

9. Place the toast on a plate and top with the strawberries and whipped coconut cream. Drizzle with maple syrup, if desired.

Ham And Cheese Cups

Servings:12
Cooking Time: 20 Minutes
Ingredients:

- 12 large eggs
- 3 tablespoons avocado oil
- 12 slices deli ham
- 1 cup shredded cheese of choice
- Salt
- Freshly ground black pepper

Directions:
1. Insert the Grill Grate and close the hood. Select GRILL, set the temperature to HI, and set the time to 20 minutes. Select START/STOP to begin preheating.
2. While the unit is preheating, in a large bowl, beat the eggs. Brush the avocado oil in the bottom and on the sides of two 6-cup muffin tins. Line each muffin cup with a slice of ham. Spoon the eggs evenly into each cup. Top with the shredded cheese and season with salt and pepper.
3. When the unit beeps to signify it has preheated, place one muffin tin on the Grill Grate. Close the hood and grill for 10 minutes.
4. After 10 minutes, open the hood and remove the muffin tin. Place the second muffin tin on the Grill Grate, close the hood, and cook for 10 minutes.
5. When cooking is complete, remove the cups from the tins and serve.

Tomato-corn Frittata With Avocado Dressing

Servings: 2 Or 3
Cooking Time: 20 Minutes
Ingredients:

- ½ cup cherry tomatoes, halved
- Kosher salt and freshly ground black pepper, to taste
- 6 large eggs, lightly beaten
- ½ cup corn kernels, thawed if frozen
- ¼ cup milk
- 1 tablespoon finely chopped fresh dill
- ½ cup shredded Monterey Jack cheese
- Avocado Dressing:
- 1 ripe avocado, pitted and peeled
- 2 tablespoons fresh lime juice
- ¼ cup olive oil
- 1 scallion, finely chopped
- 8 fresh basil leaves, finely chopped

Directions:
1. Put the tomato halves in a colander and lightly season with salt. Set aside for 10 minutes to drain well. Pour the tomatoes into a large bowl and fold in the eggs, corn, milk, and dill. Sprinkle with salt and pepper and stir until mixed.
2. Select BAKE, set the temperature to 300ºF, and set the time to 20 minutes. Select START/STOP to begin preheating.
3. Pour the egg mixture into a baking pan. Place the pan directly in the pot. Close the hood and BAKE for 15 minutes.
4. Scatter the cheese on top. Increase the grill temperature to 315ºF and continue to cook for another 5 minutes, or until the frittata is puffy and set.
5. Meanwhile, make the avocado dressing: Mash the avocado with the lime juice in a medium bowl until smooth. Mix in the olive oil, scallion, and basil and stir until well incorporated.
6. Let the frittata cool for 5 minutes and serve alongside the avocado dressing.

Cornflakes Toast Sticks

Servings: 4
Cooking Time: 6 Minutes
Ingredients:

- 2 eggs
- ½ cup milk
- ⅛ teaspoon salt
- ½ teaspoon pure vanilla extract
- ¾ cup crushed cornflakes
- 6 slices sandwich bread, each slice cut into 4 strips
- Maple syrup, for dipping
- Cooking spray

Directions:

1. Insert the Crisper Basket and close the hood. Select AIR CRISP, set the temperature to 390°F, and set the time to 6 minutes. Select START/STOP to begin preheating.
2. In a small bowl, beat together the eggs, milk, salt, and vanilla.
3. Put crushed cornflakes on a plate or in a shallow dish.
4. Dip bread strips in egg mixture, shake off excess, and roll in cornflake crumbs.
5. Spray both sides of bread strips with oil.
6. Put bread strips in Crisper Basket in a single layer.
7. Close the hood and AIR CRISP for 6 minutes or until golden brown.
8. Repeat steps 5 and 6 to AIR CRISP remaining French toast sticks.
9. Serve with maple syrup.

Banana And Oat Bread Pudding

Servings: 4
Cooking Time: 16 To 20 Minutes
Ingredients:

- 2 medium ripe bananas, mashed
- ½ cup low-fat milk
- 2 tablespoons maple syrup
- 2 tablespoons peanut butter
- 1 teaspoon vanilla extract
- 1 teaspoon ground cinnamon
- 2 slices whole-grain bread, cut into bite-sized cubes
- ¼ cup quick oats
- Cooking spray

Directions:

1. Select AIR CRISP, set the temperature to 350°F, and set the time to 20 minutes. Select START/STOP to begin preheating.
2. Spritz a baking pan lightly with cooking spray.
3. Mix the bananas, milk, maple syrup, peanut butter, vanilla, and cinnamon in a large mixing bowl and stir until well incorporated.
4. Add the bread cubes to the banana mixture and stir until thoroughly coated. Fold in the oats and stir to combine.
5. Transfer the mixture to the baking pan. Wrap the baking pan in aluminum foil.
6. Place the pan directly in the pot. Close the hood and AIR CRISP for 10 to 12 minutes until heated through.
7. Remove the foil and cook for an additional 6 to 8 minutes, or until the pudding has set.
8. Let the pudding cool for 5 minutes before serving.

Maple Walnut Pancake

Servings: 4
Cooking Time: 20 Minutes
Ingredients:

- 3 tablespoons melted butter, divided
- 1 cup flour
- 2 tablespoons sugar
- 1½ teaspoons baking powder
- ¼ teaspoon salt
- 1 egg, beaten
- ¾ cup milk
- 1 teaspoon pure vanilla extract
- ½ cup roughly chopped walnuts
- Maple syrup or fresh sliced fruit, for serving

Directions:

1. Select BAKE, set the temperature to 330°F, and set the time to 20 minutes. Select START/STOP to begin preheating.
2. Grease a baking pan with 1 tablespoon of melted butter.
3. Mix together the flour, sugar, baking powder, and salt in a medium bowl. Add the beaten egg, milk, the remaining 2 tablespoons of melted butter, and vanilla and stir until the batter is sticky but slightly lumpy.
4. Slowly pour the batter into the greased baking pan and scatter with the walnuts.
5. Place the pan directly in the pot. Close the hood and BAKE for 20 minutes until golden brown and cooked through.
6. Let the pancake rest for 5 minutes and serve topped with the maple syrup or fresh fruit, if desired.

Chocolate Banana Bread With White Chocolate

Servings: 4
Cooking Time: 30 Minutes
Ingredients:

- ¼ cup cocoa powder
- 6 tablespoons plus 2 teaspoons all-purpose flour, divided
- ½ teaspoon kosher salt
- ¼ teaspoon baking soda
- 1½ ripe bananas
- 1 large egg, whisked
- ¼ cup vegetable oil
- ½ cup sugar
- 3 tablespoons buttermilk or plain yogurt (not Greek)
- ½ teaspoon vanilla extract
- 6 tablespoons chopped white chocolate
- 6 tablespoons chopped walnuts

Directions:

1. Select BAKE, set the temperature to 310°F, and set the time to 30 minutes. Select START/STOP to begin preheating.
2. Mix together the cocoa powder, 6 tablespoons of the flour, salt, and baking soda in a medium bowl.
3. Mash the bananas with a fork in another medium bowl until smooth. Fold in the egg, oil, sugar, buttermilk, and vanilla, and whisk until thoroughly combined. Add the wet mixture to the dry mixture and stir until well incorporated.
4. Combine the white chocolate, walnuts, and the remaining 2 tablespoons of flour in a third bowl and toss to coat. Add this mixture to the batter and stir until well incorporated. Pour the batter into a baking pan and smooth the top with a spatula.
5. Place the pan directly in the pot. Close the hood and BAKE for 30 minutes. Check the bread for doneness: If a toothpick inserted into the center of the bread comes out clean, it's done.
6. Remove from the grill and allow to cool on a wire rack for 10 minutes before serving.

Crustless Broccoli Quiche

Servings: 4
Cooking Time: 10 Minutes
Ingredients:

- 1 cup broccoli florets
- ¾ cup chopped roasted red peppers
- 1¼ cups grated Fontina cheese
- 6 eggs
- ¾ cup heavy cream
- ½ teaspoon salt
- Freshly ground black pepper, to taste
- Cooking spray

Directions:

1. Select AIR CRISP, set the temperature to 325°F, and set the time to 10 minutes. Select START/STOP to begin preheating.
2. Spritz a baking pan with cooking spray
3. Add the broccoli florets and roasted red peppers to the pan and scatter the grated Fontina cheese on top.
4. In a bowl, beat together the eggs and heavy cream. Sprinkle with salt and pepper. Pour the egg mixture over the top of the cheese. Wrap the pan in foil.
5. Place the pan directly in the pot. Close the hood and AIR CRISP for 8 minutes. Remove the foil and continue to cook another 2 minutes until the quiche is golden brown.
6. Rest for 5 minutes before cutting into wedges and serve warm.

Grilled Sausage Mix

Servings: 4
Cooking Time: 22 Minutes
Ingredients:

- 8 mini bell peppers
- 2 heads radicchio, each cut into 6 wedges
- Canola oil, for brushing
- Sea salt, to taste
- Freshly ground black pepper, to taste
- 6 breakfast sausage links
- 6 hot or sweet Italian sausage links

Directions:

1. Insert the Grill Grate and close the hood. Select GRILL, set the temperature to MAX, and set the time to 22 minutes. Select START/STOP to begin preheating.
2. While the unit is preheating, brush the bell peppers and radicchio with the oil. Season with salt and black pepper.
3. When the unit beeps to signify it has preheated, place the bell peppers and radicchio on the Grill Grate; close the hood and GRILL for 10 minutes, without flipping.
4. Meanwhile, poke the sausages with a fork or knife and brush them with some of the oil.
5. After 10 minutes, remove the vegetables and set aside. Decrease the temperature to LOW. Place the sausages on the Grill Grate; close the hood and GRILL for 6 minutes.
6. Flip the sausages. Close the hood and GRILL for 6 minutes more. Remove the sausages from the Grill Grate.
7. Serve the sausages and vegetables on a large cutting board or serving tray.

Egg And Avocado Burrito

Servings: 4
Cooking Time: 3 To 5 Minutes
Ingredients:

- 4 low-sodium whole-wheat flour tortillas
- Filling:
- 1 hard-boiled egg, chopped
- 2 hard-boiled egg whites, chopped
- 1 ripe avocado, peeled, pitted, and chopped
- 1 red bell pepper, chopped
- 1 slice low-sodium, low-fat American cheese, torn into pieces
- 3 tablespoons low-sodium salsa, plus additional for serving (optional)

Directions:

1. Insert the Crisper Basket and close the hood. Select AIR CRISP, set the temperature to 390°F, and set the time to 5 minutes. Select START/STOP to begin preheating.

2. Make the filling: Combine the egg, egg whites, avocado, red bell pepper, cheese, and salsa in a medium bowl and stir until blended.

3. Assemble the burritos: Arrange the tortillas on a clean work surface and place ¼ of the prepared filling in the middle of each tortilla, leaving about 1½-inch on each end unfilled. Fold in the opposite sides of each tortilla and roll up. Secure with toothpicks through the center, if needed.

4. Transfer the burritos to the Crisper Basket. Close the hood and AIR CRISP for 3 to 5 minutes, or until the burritos are crisp and golden brown.

5. Allow to cool for 5 minutes and serve with salsa, if desired.

Stuffed Bell Peppers With Italian Maple-glazed Sausage

Servings: 6
Cooking Time: 28 Minutes
Ingredients:

- 2 pounds ground Italian sausage or links
- 1 cup light brown sugar, packed
- 6 bell peppers (any color)
- 1 cup water
- 12 tablespoons (¾ cup) maple syrup, divided

Directions:

1. Insert the Cooking Pot and close the hood. Select GRILL, set the temperature to HI, and set the time to 8 minutes. Select START/STOP to begin preheating.

2. While the unit is preheating, remove the sausage from the casings if using links.

3. When the unit beeps to signify it has preheated, place the sausage and brown sugar in the Cooking Pot. Use a wooden spoon or potato masher to break the sausage apart and mix it with the brown sugar. Close the hood and cook for 8 minutes.

4. While the sausage is cooking, cut the top off each bell pepper and remove the seeds. Then slice the bell peppers in half lengthwise.

5. When cooking is complete, spoon the sausage into each bell pepper cup. Add the water to the Cooking Pot. Place 6 bell pepper halves on the Grill Grate, and place the Grill Grate in the unit.

6. Select GRILL, set the temperature to HI, and set the time to 20 minutes. Select START/STOP and then press the PREHEAT button to skip preheating. Close the hood and cook for 5 minutes.

7. After 5 minutes, open the hood and drizzle 1 tablespoon of maple syrup in each bell pepper cup. Close the hood and cook 5 minutes more. After 5 minutes, remove the stuffed peppers and place the remaining 6 stuffed peppers on the Grill Grate. Repeat this step to cook.

8. When cooking is complete, remove the peppers from the grill and serve.

9. Adding raw sausage inside a bell pepper will result in a watery mess.

Breakfast Chilaquiles

Servings: 4
Cooking Time: 15 Minutes
Ingredients:

- 4 cups tortilla chips (40 to 50 chips)
- 1 (10- to 14-ounce) can red chile sauce or enchilada sauce
- 6 large eggs
- ¼ cup diced onion, for garnish
- ½ cup crumbled queso fresco, for garnish
- Chopped fresh cilantro, for garnish

Directions:
1. Select GRILL, set the temperature to HI, and set the time to 15 minutes. Select START/STOP to begin preheating.
2. While the unit is preheating, add the tortilla chips to the Cooking Pot and pour the red chile sauce over them.
3. When the unit beeps to signify it has preheated, place the Cooking Pot in the unit. Crack the eggs, one at a time, over the tortilla chips, making sure they're evenly spread out. Close the hood and cook for 15 minutes.
4. Cooking is complete when the egg whites are firm with a runny yellow center. Garnish with the onion, queso fresco, and fresh cilantro, and serve.

Ham And Corn Muffins

Servings:8
Cooking Time: 6 Minutes
Ingredients:

- ¾ cup yellow cornmeal
- ¼ cup flour
- 1½ teaspoons baking powder
- ¼ teaspoon salt
- 1 egg, beaten
- 2 tablespoons canola oil
- ½ cup milk
- ½ cup shredded sharp Cheddar cheese
- ½ cup diced ham

Directions:
1. Select BAKE, set the temperature to 390°F, and set the time to 6 minutes. Select START/STOP to begin preheating.
2. In a medium bowl, stir together the cornmeal, flour, baking powder, and salt.
3. Add the egg, oil, and milk to dry ingredients and mix well.
4. Stir in shredded cheese and diced ham.
5. Divide batter among 8 parchment paper-lined muffin cups.
6. Put 4 filled muffin cups in the pot. Close the hood and BAKE for 5 minutes.
7. Reduce temperature to 330°F and bake for 1 minute or until a toothpick inserted in center of the muffin comes out clean.
8. Repeat steps 6 and 7 to bake remaining muffins.
9. Serve warm.

Honey-lime Glazed Grilled Fruit Salad

Servings: 4
Cooking Time: 4 Minutes
Ingredients:

- ½ pound strawberries, washed, hulled and halved
- 1 can pineapple chunks, drained, juice reserved
- 2 peaches, pitted and sliced
- 6 tablespoons honey, divided
- 1 tablespoon freshly squeezed lime juice

Directions:
1. Insert the Grill Grate and close the hood. Select GRILL, set the temperature to MAX, and set the time to 4 minutes. Select START/STOP to begin preheating.
2. While the unit is preheating, combine the strawberries, pineapple, and peaches in a large bowl with 3 tablespoons of honey. Toss to coat evenly.
3. When the unit beeps to signify it has preheated, place the fruit on the Grill Grate. Gently press the fruit down to maximize grill marks. Close the hood and GRILL for 4 minutes without flipping.
4. Meanwhile, in a small bowl, combine the remaining 3 tablespoons of honey, lime juice, and 1 tablespoon of reserved pineapple juice.
5. When cooking is complete, place the fruit in a large bowl and toss with the honey mixture. Serve immediately.

Mixed Berry Dutch Baby Pancake

Servings: 4
Cooking Time: 12 To 16 Minutes

Ingredients:

- 1 tablespoon unsalted butter, at room temperature
- 1 egg
- 2 egg whites
- ½ cup 2% milk
- ½ cup whole-wheat pastry flour
- 1 teaspoon pure vanilla extract
- 1 cup sliced fresh strawberries
- ½ cup fresh raspberries
- ½ cup fresh blueberries

Directions:

1. Select BAKE, set the temperature to 330°F, and set the time to 16 minutes. Select START/STOP to begin preheating.
2. Grease a baking pan with the butter.
3. Using a hand mixer, beat together the egg, egg whites, milk, pastry flour, and vanilla in a medium mixing bowl until well incorporated.
4. Pour the batter into the pan. Place the pan directly in the pot. Close the hood and BAKE for 12 to 16 minutes, or until the pancake puffs up in the center and the edges are golden brown.
5. Allow the pancake to cool for 5 minutes and serve topped with the berries.

Blueberry Dump Cake

Servings: 6 To 8
Cooking Time: 25 Minutes

Ingredients:

- 3 cups fresh blueberries
- ½ cup granulated sugar
- 1 (16-ounce) box yellow cake mix
- 8 tablespoons (1 stick) unsalted butter, melted

Directions:

1. Select BAKE, set the temperature to 300°F, and set the time to 25 minutes. Select START/STOP to begin preheating.
2. While the unit is preheating, wash and pat dry the blueberries. Then place them and the sugar into the Cooking Pot and mix to coat the fruit with the sugar.
3. In a large bowl, mix together the cake mix and melted butter. Stir until the cake mix is no longer a powder but crumbly like a streusel. Cover the blueberry-sugar mixture with the cake crumble.
4. When the unit beeps to signify it has preheated, place the Cooking Pot in the unit. Close the hood and bake for 25 minutes.
5. Baking is complete when the fresh blueberries have bubbled and the cake crumble is golden brown. Serve.

Mini Caprese Pizzas

Servings: 4
Cooking Time: 10 Minutes

Ingredients:

- 1 (14-ounce) package refrigerated pizza dough
- 2 tablespoons extra-virgin olive oil
- 2 large tomatoes, thinly sliced
- 8 ounces fresh mozzarella cheese, cut into thin discs
- 12 fresh basil leaves
- Balsamic vinegar, for drizzling or dipping

Directions:

1. Insert the Grill Grate and close the hood. Select GRILL, set the temperature to MED, and set the time to 10 minutes. Select START/STOP to begin preheating.
2. While the unit is preheating, lay the pizza dough on a flat surface. Cut out 12 small round pizzas 1½ to 2 inches diameter each. Brush both sides of each dough round with the olive oil.
3. When the unit beeps to signify it has preheated, place the dough rounds on the Grill Grate, 4 across, in 3 rows. Close the hood and grill for 5 minutes.
4. After 5 minutes, open the hood and flip the rounds. Top each round with the tomato and cheese slices. Close the hood and cook for 5 minutes more.
5. When cooking is complete, remove the pizzas from the Grill Grate. Top each with the basil. When ready to serve, drizzle each pizza with the balsamic vinegar, or keep the vinegar on the side in a small bowl for dipping.

Chicken Breakfast Sausages

Servings:8
Cooking Time: 8 To 12 Minutes

Ingredients:

- 1 Granny Smith apple, peeled and finely chopped
- 2 tablespoons apple juice
- 2 garlic cloves, minced
- 1 egg white
- ⅓ cup minced onion
- 3 tablespoons ground almonds
- ⅛ teaspoon freshly ground black pepper
- 1 pound ground chicken breast

Directions:

1. Insert the Crisper Basket and close the hood. Select AIR CRISP, set the temperature to 330°F, and set the time to 12 minutes. Select START/STOP to begin preheating.
2. Combine all the ingredients except the chicken in a medium mixing bowl and stir well.
3. Add the chicken breast to the apple mixture and mix with your hands until well incorporated.
4. Divide the mixture into 8 equal portions and shape into patties. Arrange the patties in the Crisper Basket. You may need to work in batches depending on the size of your Crisper Basket.
5. Close the hood and AIR CRISP for 8 to 12 minutes, or until a meat thermometer inserted in the center of the chicken reaches at least 165°F.
6. Remove from the grill to a plate and repeat with the remaining patties.
7. Let the chicken cool for 5 minutes and serve warm.

Fluffy Pancake Sheet

Servings: 4
Cooking Time: 12 Minutes

Ingredients:

- 3 cups pancake mix
- 1½ cups milk
- 2 eggs
- Nonstick cooking spray
- Unsalted butter, for topping
- Maple syrup, for topping

Directions:

1. Insert the Cooking Pot and close the hood. Select BAKE, set the temperature to 350°F, and set the time to 12 minutes. Select START/STOP to begin preheating.
2. While the unit is preheating, in a large bowl, whisk together the pancake mix, milk, and eggs.
3. When the unit beeps to signify it has preheated, spray the Cooking Pot with cooking spray. Pour the batter into the pot. Close the hood and cook for 12 minutes.
4. When cooking is complete, cut the pancake into squares. Top with the butter and maple syrup and serve.

Sourdough Croutons

Servings:4
Cooking Time: 6 Minutes

Ingredients:

- 4 cups cubed sourdough bread, 1-inch cubes
- 1 tablespoon olive oil
- 1 teaspoon fresh thyme leaves
- ¼ teaspoon salt
- Freshly ground black pepper, to taste

Directions:

1. Combine all ingredients in a bowl.
2. Insert the Crisper Basket and close the hood. Select AIR CRISP, set the temperature to 400°F, and set the time to 6 minutes. Select START/STOP to begin preheating.
3. Toss the bread cubes and transfer to the basket. Close the hood and AIR CRISP for 6 minutes, shaking the basket once or twice while they cook.
4. Serve warm.

Avocado Quesadillas

Servings: 4
Cooking Time: 11 Minutes
Ingredients:

- 4 eggs
- 2 tablespoons skim milk
- Salt and ground black pepper, to taste
- Cooking spray
-

- 4 flour tortillas
- 4 tablespoons salsa
- 2 ounces Cheddar cheese, grated
- ½ small avocado, peeled and thinly sliced

Directions:

1. Select BAKE, set the temperature to 270°F, and set the time to 8 minutes. Select START/STOP to begin preheating.
2. Beat together the eggs, milk, salt, and pepper.
3. Spray a baking pan lightly with cooking spray and add egg mixture.
4. Place the pan directly in the pot. Close the hood and BAKE for 8 minutes, stirring every 1 to 2 minutes, until eggs are scrambled to the liking. Remove and set aside.
5. Spray one side of each tortilla with cooking spray. Flip over.
6. Divide eggs, salsa, cheese, and avocado among the tortillas, covering only half of each tortilla.
7. Fold each tortilla in half and press down lightly. Increase the temperature of the grill to 390°F.
8. Put 2 tortillas in Crisper Basket and AIR CRISP for 3 minutes or until cheese melts and outside feels slightly crispy. Repeat with remaining two tortillas.
9. Cut each cooked tortilla into halves. Serve warm.

Asparagus And Cheese Strata

Servings: 4
Cooking Time: 14 To 19 Minutes
Ingredients:

- 6 asparagus spears, cut into 2-inch pieces
- 1 tablespoon water
- 2 slices whole-wheat bread, cut into ½-inch cubes
- 4 eggs
- 3 tablespoons whole milk

- 2 tablespoons chopped flat-leaf parsley
- ½ cup grated Havarti or Swiss cheese
- Pinch salt
- Freshly ground black pepper, to taste
- Cooking spray

Directions:

1. Select BAKE, set the temperature to 330°F, and set the time to 19 minutes. Select START/STOP to begin preheating.
2. Add the asparagus spears and 1 tablespoon of water in a baking pan. Place the pan directly in the pot. Close the hood and BAKE for 3 to 5 minutes until crisp-tender. Remove the asparagus from the pan and drain on paper towels. Spritz the pan with cooking spray.
3. Place the bread and asparagus in the pan.
4. Whisk together the eggs and milk in a medium mixing bowl until creamy. Fold in the parsley, cheese, salt, and pepper and stir to combine. Pour this mixture into the baking pan.
5. Place the pan directly in the pot. Close the hood and BAKE for 11 to 14 minutes, or until the eggs are set and the top is lightly browned.
6. Let cool for 5 minutes before slicing and serving.

Banana Bread

Servings:3
Cooking Time: 22 Minutes
Ingredients:

- 3 ripe bananas, mashed
- 1 cup sugar
- 1 large egg
- 4 tablespoons (½ stick) unsalted butter, melted
- 1½ cups all-purpose flour
- 1 teaspoon baking soda
- 1 teaspoon salt

Directions:

1. Coat the insides of 3 mini loaf pans with cooking spray.
2. In a large mixing bowl, mix the bananas and sugar.
3. In a separate large mixing bowl, combine the egg, butter, flour, baking soda, and salt and mix well.
4. Add the banana mixture to the egg and flour mixture. Mix well.
5. Divide the batter evenly among the prepared pans.
6. Select BAKE, set the temperature to 310°F, and set the time to 22 minutes. Select START/STOP to begin preheating.
7. Set the mini loaf pans into the pot.
8. Close the hood and BAKE for 22 minutes. Insert a toothpick into the center of each loaf; if it comes out clean, they are done.
9. When the loaves are cooked through, remove the pans from the Crisper Basket. Turn out the loaves onto a wire rack to cool.
10. Serve warm.

Mushroom And Squash Toast

Servings: 4
Cooking Time: 10 Minutes
Ingredients:

- 1 tablespoon olive oil
- 1 red bell pepper, cut into strips
- 2 green onions, sliced
- 1 cup sliced button or cremini mushrooms
- 1 small yellow squash, sliced
- 2 tablespoons softened butter
- 4 slices bread
- ½ cup soft goat cheese

Directions:

1. Brush the Crisper Basket with the olive oil.
2. Insert the Crisper Basket and close the hood. Select AIR CRISP, set the temperature to 350°F, and set the time to 7 minutes. Select START/STOP to begin preheating.
3. Put the red pepper, green onions, mushrooms, and squash inside the basket and give them a stir. Close the hood and AIR CRISP for 7 minutes or the vegetables are tender, shaking the basket once throughout the cooking time.
4. Remove the vegetables and set them aside.
5. Spread the butter on the slices of bread and transfer to the basket, butter-side up. Close the hood and AIR CRISP for 3 minutes.
6. Remove the toast from the grill and top with goat cheese and vegetables. Serve warm.

Country-fried Steak And Eggs

Servings: 4
Cooking Time: 16 Minutes
Ingredients:

- For the country-fried steak
- 1 cup milk
- 2 large eggs
- 2 cups all-purpose flour
- 2 teaspoons salt
- 1 teaspoon freshly ground black pepper
- 1 teaspoon garlic powder
- 1 teaspoon onion powder
- ¼ teaspoon cayenne pepper
- ¾ teaspoon paprika
- 4 (8-ounce) cube or round steaks
- For the eggs and gravy
- 4 to 8 large eggs
- 4 tablespoons (½ stick) unsalted butter
- 4 tablespoons all-purpose flour
- ½ cup heavy (whipping) cream
- ¼ teaspoon salt
- ¼ teaspoon freshly ground black pepper

Directions:
1. Create an assembly line with 3 shallow dishes. In the first dish, whisk together the milk and eggs. In the second dish, combine the flour, salt, black pepper, garlic powder, onion powder, cayenne pepper, and paprika. Place a steak in the flour mixture to coat both sides, then dip it into the egg mixture to coat both sides. Dip the steak back in the flour mixture, coating both sides. Place the coated steaks in the third shallow dish.
2. Insert the Grill Grate and close the hood. Select GRILL, set the temperature to HI, and set the time to 6 minutes. Select START/STOP to begin preheating.
3. When the unit beeps to signify it has preheated, place all 4 steaks on the Grill Grate. Close the hood and cook for 3 minutes.
4. After 3 minutes, open the hood and flip the steaks. Close the hood and cook for 3 minutes more.
5. When grilling is complete, transfer the steaks to a plate. Using grill mitts, remove the Grill Grate from the unit, leaving any excess fat drippings from the Grill Grate in the Cooking Pot.
6. Select AIR CRISP, set the temperature to 400°F, and set the time to 10 minutes. Select START/STOP and then press the PREHEAT button to skip preheating. Crack the eggs in the Cooking Pot. Close the hood and cook for 5 minutes, until the egg whites are opaque and firm. Remove the eggs from the pot.
7. Place the butter and flour in the Cooking Pot with the remaining fat drippings. Stir with a wooden spoon or silicone whisk until the butter has melted. Pour in the heavy cream and add the salt and pepper. Stir until completely mixed.
8. Close the hood and cook for 3 minutes. After 3 minutes, open the hood, stir the gravy, then close the hood to cook for 2 minutes more.
9. When cooking is complete, stir the gravy again and let it sit until you're ready to serve. To serve, pour the gravy over the country-fried steaks next to the eggs.

Pesto Egg Croissantwiches

Servings: 4
Cooking Time: 8 Minutes
Ingredients:

- 4 large eggs
- 4 croissants
- 8 tablespoons pesto

Directions:
1. Insert the Cooking Pot and close the hood. Select GRILL, set the temperature to HI, and set the time to 8 minutes. Select START/STOP to begin preheating.
2. While the unit is preheating, in a small bowl, whisk together the eggs.
3. When the unit beeps to signify it has preheated, pour the beaten eggs into the Cooking Pot. Close the hood and cook for 4 minutes.
4. While the eggs are cooking, split the croissants. Place the croissant halves on top of the Grill Grate.
5. After 4 minutes, open the hood and scramble the eggs with a spatula. Spoon the scrambled eggs onto the bottom halves of the croissants. Remove the Cooking Pot from the unit.
6. Insert the Grill Grate into the unit. Spoon 2 tablespoons of pesto on top of each egg-topped croissant, then top each sandwich with the croissant top. Close the hood and cook for 4 minutes.
7. When cooking is complete, the croissant crust should be toasted. Serve.

Cheesy Breakfast Casserole

Servings: 4
Cooking Time: 14 Minutes

Ingredients:

- 6 slices bacon
- 6 eggs
- Salt and pepper, to taste
- Cooking spray
- ½ cup chopped green bell pepper
- ½ cup chopped onion
- ¾ cup shredded Cheddar cheese

Directions:

1. Place the bacon in a skillet over medium-high heat and cook each side for about 4 minutes until evenly crisp. Remove from the heat to a paper towel-lined plate to drain. Crumble it into small pieces and set aside.
2. Whisk the eggs with the salt and pepper in a medium bowl.
3. Select BAKE, set the temperature to 400°F, and set the time to 8 minutes. Select START/STOP to begin preheating.
4. Spritz a baking pan with cooking spray.
5. Place the whisked eggs, crumbled bacon, green bell pepper, and onion in the prepared pan. Place the pan directly in the pot. Close the hood and BAKE for 6 minutes.
6. Scatter the Cheddar cheese all over and bake for 2 minutes more.
7. Allow to sit for 5 minutes and serve on plates.

Bacon And Egg Bread Cups

Servings: 4
Cooking Time: 8 To 12 Minutes

Ingredients:

- 4 crusty rolls
- 4 thin slices Gouda or Swiss cheese mini wedges
- 5 eggs
- 2 tablespoons heavy cream
- 3 strips precooked bacon, chopped
- ½ teaspoon dried thyme
- Pinch salt
- Freshly ground black pepper, to taste

Directions:

1. Select BAKE, set the temperature to 330°F, and set the time to 12 minutes. Select START/STOP to begin preheating.
2. On a clean work surface, cut the tops off the rolls. Using your fingers, remove the insides of the rolls to make bread cups, leaving a ½-inch shell. Place a slice of cheese onto each roll bottom.
3. Whisk together the eggs and heavy cream in a medium bowl until well combined. Fold in the bacon, thyme, salt, and pepper and stir well.
4. Scrape the egg mixture into the prepared bread cups.
5. Place the bread cups directly in the pot. Close the hood and BAKE for 8 to 12 minutes, or until the eggs are cooked to your preference.
6. Serve warm.

Meatless Recipes

Italian Baked Tofu

Servings: 2
Cooking Time: 10 Minutes
Ingredients:

- 1 tablespoon soy sauce
- 1 tablespoon water
- ⅓ teaspoon garlic powder
- ⅓ teaspoon onion powder
- ⅓ teaspoon dried oregano
- ⅓ teaspoon dried basil
- Black pepper, to taste
- 6 ounces extra firm tofu, pressed and cubed

Directions:

1. In a large mixing bowl, whisk together the soy sauce, water, garlic powder, onion powder, oregano, basil, and black pepper. Add the tofu cubes, stirring to coat, and let them marinate for 10 minutes.
2. Select BAKE, set the temperature to 390°F, and set the time to 10 minutes. Select START/STOP to begin preheating.
3. Arrange the tofu in the baking pan. Place the pan directly in the pot. Close the hood and BAKE for 10 minutes until crisp. Flip the tofu halfway through the cooking time.
4. Remove from the basket to a plate and serve.

Eggplant Parmigiana

Servings: 4
Cooking Time: 12 Minutes
Ingredients:

- 2 large eggs
- ½ cup grated Parmesan cheese, plus more for garnish
- 1 tablespoon Italian seasoning
- 1 teaspoon garlic powder
- 2 Italian eggplants, cut into ¾-inch-thick discs
- ½ cup ricotta cheese
- 1 cup prepared marinara sauce
- ½ cup shredded mozzarella cheese
- Fresh basil, for garnish

Directions:

1. Insert the Grill Grate and close the hood. Select GRILL, set the temperature to HI, and set the time to 12 minutes. Select START/STOP to begin preheating.
2. While the unit is preheating, create an assembly line with 2 large bowls. In one bowl, whisk the eggs. In the other bowl, combine the Parmesan cheese, Italian seasoning, and garlic powder. Dip the eggplant discs in the egg wash and then into the Parmesan crumbs until fully coated.
3. When the unit beeps to signify it has preheated, place the eggplant on the Grill Grate in a single layer. Close the hood and grill for 4 minutes.
4. After 4 minutes, open the hood and flip the eggplant. Close the hood and cook for 4 minutes.
5. After 4 minutes, open the hood and use grill mitts to remove the Grill Grate and eggplant.
6. Place an eggplant disc in the Cooking Pot. Spoon about 1 teaspoon of ricotta cheese across the disc and then top with another eggplant disc, forming a sandwich. Add a teaspoon of marinara sauce on top, followed by shredded mozzarella cheese. Repeat with the remaining eggplant discs, ricotta cheese, marinara sauce, and mozzarella cheese. Close the hood and cook for 4 minutes more.
7. When cooking is complete, remove the eggplant. Garnish with fresh basil leaves and top with more grated Parmesan, and serve.

Spicy Cauliflower Roast

Servings: 4

Cooking Time: 20 Minutes

Ingredients:

- Cauliflower:
- 5 cups cauliflower florets
- 3 tablespoons vegetable oil
- ½ teaspoon ground cumin
- ½ teaspoon ground coriander
- ½ teaspoon kosher salt
- Sauce:
- ½ cup Greek yogurt or sour cream
- ¼ cup chopped fresh cilantro
- 1 jalapeño, coarsely chopped
- 4 cloves garlic, peeled
- ½ teaspoon kosher salt
- 2 tablespoons water

Directions:

1. Insert the Crisper Basket and close the hood. Select ROAST, set the temperature to 400°F, and set the time to 20 minutes. Select START/STOP to begin preheating.

2. In a large bowl, combine the cauliflower, oil, cumin, coriander, and salt. Toss to coat.

3. Put the cauliflower in the Crisper Basket. Close the hood and ROAST for 20 minutes, stirring halfway through the roasting time.

4. Meanwhile, in a blender, combine the yogurt, cilantro, jalapeño, garlic, and salt. Blend, adding the water as needed to keep the blades moving and to thin the sauce.

5. At the end of roasting time, transfer the cauliflower to a large serving bowl. Pour the sauce over and toss gently to coat. Serve immediately.

Honey-sriracha Brussels Sprouts

Servings: 8

Cooking Time: 20 Minutes

Ingredients:

- 2 pounds Brussels sprouts, halved lengthwise, ends trimmed
- 2 tablespoons avocado oil
- 4 tablespoons honey or coconut palm sugar
- 2 teaspoons sriracha
- Juice of 1 lemon

Directions:

1. Insert the Crisper Basket and close the hood. Select AIR CRISP, set the temperature to 390°F, and set the time to 20 minutes. Select START/STOP to begin preheating.

2. While the unit is preheating, in a large bowl, toss the Brussels sprouts with the avocado oil.

3. When the unit beeps to signify it has preheated, place the Brussels sprouts in the Crisper Basket. Close the hood and cook for 10 minutes.

4. After 10 minutes, open the hood and toss the Brussels sprouts. Close the hood and cook for 10 minutes more. If you choose, before the last 5 minutes, open the hood and toss the Brussels sprouts one more time.

5. When cooking is complete, open the hood and transfer the Brussels sprouts to a large bowl. Or if you like more crisping and browning of your sprouts, continue cooking to your liking.

6. In a small bowl, whisk together the honey, sriracha, and lemon juice. Drizzle this over the Brussels sprouts and toss to coat. Serve.

Grilled Mozzarella Eggplant Stacks

Servings: 4
Cooking Time: 14 Minutes

Ingredients:

- 1 eggplant, sliced ¼-inch thick
- 2 tablespoons canola oil
- 2 beefsteak or heirloom tomatoes, sliced ¼-inch thick
- 12 large basil leaves
- ½ pound buffalo Mozzarella, sliced ¼-inch thick
- Sea salt, to taste

Directions:

1. Insert the Grill Grate and close the hood. Select GRILL, set the temperature to MAX, and set the time to 14 minutes. Select START/STOP to begin preheating.
2. Meanwhile, in a large bowl, toss the eggplant and oil until evenly coated.
3. When the unit beeps to signify it has preheated, place the eggplant on the Grill Grate. Close the hood and GRILL for 8 to 12 minutes, until charred on all sides.
4. After 8 to 12 minutes, top the eggplant with one slice each of tomato and Mozzarella. Close the hood and GRILL for 2 minutes, until the cheese melts.
5. When cooking is complete, remove the eggplant stacks from the grill. Place 2 or 3 basil leaves on top of half of the stacks. Place the remaining eggplant stacks on top of those with basil so that there are four stacks total. Season with salt, garnish with the remaining basil, and serve.

Broccoli And Tofu Teriyaki

Servings: 4
Cooking Time: 8 Minutes

Ingredients:

- 1 (14-ounce) package firm tofu, cut into ½-inch cubes
- 1 medium head broccoli, chopped into florets (3 to 4 cups)
- Extra-virgin olive oil
- 1 cup water
- ⅓ cup soy sauce
- 3 tablespoons light brown sugar, packed
- 1 tablespoon peeled minced fresh ginger
- ¼ teaspoon garlic powder
- 1 teaspoon cornstarch

Directions:

1. Insert the Grill Grate and close the hood. Select GRILL, set the temperature to HI, and set the time to 8 minutes. Select START/STOP to begin preheating.
2. While the unit is preheating, on a large plate, lightly coat the tofu and broccoli florets with extra-virgin olive oil.
3. When the unit beeps to signify it has preheated, place the broccoli and tofu pieces on the Grill Grate. Close the hood and grill for 4 minutes.
4. While the tofu and broccoli are cooking, in a small bowl, mix together the water, soy sauce, brown sugar, ginger, garlic powder, and cornstarch until the sugar and cornstarch are dissolved.
5. After 4 minutes, open the hood and use grill mitts to remove the Grill Grate and the broccoli and tofu. Carefully pour the soy sauce mix into the Cooking Pot and add the broccoli and tofu. Close the hood and cook for 4 minutes more.
6. When cooking is complete, open the hood and stir. Serve.

Cheese And Spinach Stuffed Portobellos

Servings: 4
Cooking Time: 8 Minutes
Ingredients:

- 4 large portobello mushrooms, rinsed, stemmed, and gills removed
- 4 ounces cream cheese, at room temperature
- ½ cup mayonnaise
- ½ cup sour cream
- 1 teaspoon onion powder
- ¼ teaspoon garlic powder
- ¼ cup grated Parmesan cheese
- ½ cup shredded mozzarella cheese
- 2 cups fresh spinach

Directions:

1. Insert the Grill Grate and close the hood. Select GRILL, set the temperature to HI, and set the time to 8 minutes. Select START/STOP to begin preheating.
2. When the unit beeps to signify it has preheated, place the mushrooms on the Grill Grate, cap-side up. Close the hood and cook for 4 minutes.
3. While the mushrooms are grilling, in a large bowl, combine the cream cheese, mayonnaise, sour cream, onion powder, garlic powder, Parmesan cheese, mozzarella cheese, and spinach. Mix well.
4. After 4 minutes, open the hood and flip the mushrooms. Evenly distribute the filling inside the caps. Close the hood and cook for 4 minutes more.
5. When cooking is complete, remove the stuffed mushrooms from the grill and serve.

Grilled Mozzarella And Tomatoes

Servings: 4
Cooking Time: 5 Minutes
Ingredients:

- 4 large, round, firm tomatoes
- ½ cup Italian dressing
- 1 cup shredded mozzarella
- ½ cup chopped fresh basil, for garnish

Directions:

1. Insert the Grill Grate and close the hood. Select GRILL, set the temperature to HI, and set the time to 5 minutes. Select START/STOP to begin preheating.
2. While the unit is preheating, cut the tomatoes in half crosswise. Pour about 1 tablespoon of Italian dressing on each tomato half.
3. When the unit beeps to signify it has preheated, place the tomatoes on the Grill Grate, cut-side up. If the tomatoes won't stand upright, slice a small piece from the bottom to level them out. Close the hood and grill for 2 minutes.
4. After 2 minutes, open the hood and evenly distribute the mozzarella cheese on top of the tomatoes. Close the hood and cook for 3 minutes more, or until the cheese is melted.
5. When cooking is complete, remove the tomatoes from the grill. Garnish with the basil and serve.

Rosemary Roasted Potatoes

Servings: 4
Cooking Time: 20 To 22 Minutes
Ingredients:

- 1½ pounds small red potatoes, cut into 1-inch cubes
- 2 tablespoons olive oil
- 2 tablespoons minced fresh rosemary
- 1 tablespoon minced garlic
- 1 teaspoon salt, plus additional as needed
- ½ teaspoon freshly ground black pepper, plus additional as needed

Directions:

1. Insert the Crisper Basket and close the hood. Select ROAST, set the temperature to 400°F, and set the time to 22 minutes. Select START/STOP to begin preheating.
2. Toss the potato cubes with the olive oil, rosemary, garlic, salt, and pepper in a large bowl until thoroughly coated.
3. Arrange the potato cubes in the Crisper Basket in a single layer. Close the hood and ROAST for 20 to 22 minutes until the potatoes are tender. Shake the basket a few times during cooking for even cooking.
4. Remove from the basket to a plate. Taste and add additional salt and pepper as needed.

Perfect Grilled Asparagus

Servings: 4
Cooking Time: 6 Minutes
Ingredients:

- 24 asparagus spears, woody ends trimmed
- Extra-virgin olive oil, for drizzling
- Sea salt
- Freshly ground black pepper

Directions:

1. Insert the Grill Grate and close the hood. Select GRILL, set the temperature to HI, and set the time to 6 minutes. Select START/STOP to begin preheating.
2. While the unit is preheating, place the asparagus in a large bowl and drizzle with the olive oil. Toss to coat, then season with salt and pepper.
3. When the unit beeps to signify it has preheated, place the spears evenly spread out on the Grill Grate. Close the hood and grill for 3 minutes.
4. After 3 minutes, open the hood and flip and move the spears around. Close the hood and cook for 3 minutes more.
5. When cooking is complete, remove the asparagus from the grill and serve.

Loaded Zucchini Boats

Servings: 4
Cooking Time: 10 Minutes
Ingredients:

- 4 medium zucchini
- 1 cup panko bread crumbs
- 2 garlic cloves, minced
- ½ small white onion, diced
- ½ cup grated Parmesan cheese
- 1 tablespoon Italian seasoning

Directions:

1. Insert the Grill Grate and close the hood. Select GRILL, set the temperature to HI, and set the time to 10 minutes. Select START/STOP to begin preheating.
2. While the unit is preheating, cut the zucchini in half lengthwise. Carefully scoop out the flesh and put it in a medium bowl. Set the boats aside.
3. Add the panko bread crumbs, garlic, onion, Parmesan cheese, and Italian seasoning to the bowl and mix well. Spoon the filling into each zucchini half.
4. When the unit beeps to signify it has preheated, place the zucchini boats on the Grill Grate, cut-side up. Close the hood and grill for 10 minutes.
5. When cooking is complete, the cheese will be melted and the tops will be crispy and golden brown. Remove the zucchini boats from the grill and serve.

Rosemary Roasted Squash With Cheese

Servings: 2
Cooking Time: 20 Minutes
Ingredients:

- 1 pound butternut squash, cut into wedges
- 2 tablespoons olive oil
- 1 tablespoon dried rosemary
- Salt, to salt
- 1 cup crumbled goat cheese
- 1 tablespoon maple syrup

Directions:

1. Insert the Crisper Basket and close the hood. Select ROAST, set the temperature to 350°F, and set the time to 20 minutes. Select START/STOP to begin preheating.
2. Toss the squash wedges with the olive oil, rosemary, and salt in a large bowl until well coated.
3. Transfer the squash wedges to the Crisper Basket, spreading them out in as even a layer as possible.
4. Close the hood and ROAST for 10 minutes. Flip the squash and roast for another 10 minutes until golden brown.
5. Sprinkle the goat cheese on top and serve drizzled with the maple syrup.

Cheesy Asparagus And Potato Platter

Servings: 5
Cooking Time: 26 To 30 Minutes
Ingredients:

- 4 medium potatoes, cut into wedges
- Cooking spray
- 1 bunch asparagus, trimmed
- 2 tablespoons olive oil
- Salt and pepper, to taste
- Cheese Sauce:
- ¼ cup crumbled cottage cheese
- ¼ cup buttermilk
- 1 tablespoon whole-grain mustard
- Salt and black pepper, to taste

Directions:

1. Insert the Crisper Basket and close the hood. Select ROAST, set the temperature to 400°F, and set the time to 30 minutes. Select START/STOP to begin preheating.
2. Spritz the Crisper Basket with cooking spray.
3. Put the potatoes in the Crisper Basket. Close the hood and ROAST for 20 to 22 minutes, until golden brown. Shake the basket halfway through the cooking time.
4. When ready, remove the potatoes from the basket to a platter. Cover the potatoes with foil to keep warm. Set aside.
5. Place the asparagus in the Crisper Basket and drizzle with the olive oil. Sprinkle with salt and pepper.
6. Close the hood and ROAST for 6 to 8 minutes, shaking the basket once or twice during cooking, or until the asparagus is cooked to your desired crispiness.
7. Meanwhile, make the cheese sauce by stirring together the cottage cheese, buttermilk, and mustard in a small bowl. Season with salt and pepper.
8. Transfer the asparagus to the platter of potatoes and drizzle with the cheese sauce. Serve immediately.

Fast And Easy Asparagus

Servings: 4
Cooking Time: 5 Minutes
Ingredients:

- 1 pound fresh asparagus spears, trimmed
- 1 tablespoon olive oil
- Salt and ground black pepper, to taste

Directions:

1. Insert the Crisper Basket and close the hood. Select AIR CRISP, set the temperature to 375°F, and set the time to 5 minutes. Select START/STOP to begin preheating.
2. Combine all the ingredients and transfer to the Crisper Basket.
3. Close the hood and AIR CRISP for 5 minutes or until soft.
4. Serve hot.

Buttered Broccoli With Parmesan

Servings: 4
Cooking Time: 4 Minutes
Ingredients:

- 1 pound broccoli florets
- 1 medium shallot, minced
- 2 tablespoons olive oil
- 2 tablespoons unsalted butter, melted
- 2 teaspoons minced garlic
- ¼ cup grated Parmesan cheese

Directions:

1. Insert the Crisper Basket and close the hood. Select ROAST, set the temperature to 360°F, and set the time to 4 minutes. Select START/STOP to begin preheating.
2. Combine the broccoli florets with the shallot, olive oil, butter, garlic, and Parmesan cheese in a medium bowl and toss until the broccoli florets are thoroughly coated.
3. Arrange the broccoli florets in the Crisper Basket in a single layer. Close the hood and ROAST for 4 minutes until crisp-tender.
4. Serve warm.

Cauliflower Steaks With Ranch Dressing

Servings: 2
Cooking Time: 15 Minutes
Ingredients:

- 1 head cauliflower, stemmed and leaves removed
- ¼ cup canola oil
- ½ teaspoon garlic powder
- ½ teaspoon paprika
- Sea salt, to taste
- Freshly ground black pepper, to taste
- 1 cup shredded Cheddar cheese
- Ranch dressing, for garnish
- 4 slices bacon, cooked and crumbled
- 2 tablespoons chopped fresh chives

Directions:

1. Cut the cauliflower from top to bottom into two 2-inch "steaks"; reserve the remaining cauliflower to cook separately.
2. Insert the Grill Grate and close the hood. Select GRILL, set the temperature to MAX, and set the time to 15 minutes. Select START/STOP to begin preheating.
3. Meanwhile, in a small bowl, whisk together the oil, garlic powder, and paprika. Season with salt and pepper. Brush each steak with the oil mixture on both sides.
4. When the unit beeps to signify it has preheated, place the steaks on the Grill Grate. Close the hood and GRILL for 10 minutes.
5. After 10 minutes, flip the steaks and top each with ½ cup of cheese. Close the hood and continue to GRILL until the cheese is melted, about 5 minutes.
6. When cooking is complete, place the cauliflower steaks on a plate and drizzle with the ranch dressing. Top with the bacon and chives.

Cheesy Macaroni Balls

Servings: 2
Cooking Time: 10 Minutes
Ingredients:

- 2 cups leftover macaroni
- 1 cup shredded Cheddar cheese
- ½ cup flour
- 1 cup bread crumbs
- 3 large eggs
- 1 cup milk
- ½ teaspoon salt
- ¼ teaspoon black pepper

Directions:

1. Insert the Crisper Basket and close the hood. Select AIR CRISP, set the temperature to 365°F, and set the time to 10 minutes. Select START/STOP to begin preheating.
2. In a bowl, combine the leftover macaroni and shredded cheese.
3. Pour the flour in a separate bowl. Put the bread crumbs in a third bowl. Finally, in a fourth bowl, mix the eggs and milk with a whisk.
4. With an ice-cream scoop, create balls from the macaroni mixture. Coat them the flour, then in the egg mixture, and lastly in the bread crumbs.
5. Arrange the balls in the basket. Close the hood and AIR CRISP for 10 minutes, giving them an occasional stir. Ensure they crisp up nicely.
6. Serve hot.

Corn Pakodas

Servings: 5
Cooking Time: 8 Minutes
Ingredients:

- 1 cup flour
- ¼ teaspoon baking soda
- ¼ teaspoon salt
- ½ teaspoon curry powder
- ½ teaspoon red chili powder
- ¼ teaspoon turmeric powder
- ¼ cup water
- 10 cobs baby corn, blanched
- Cooking spray

Directions:

1. Insert the Crisper Basket and close the hood. Select AIR CRISP, set the temperature to 425°F, and set the time to 8 minutes. Select START/STOP to begin preheating.
2. Cover the Crisper Basket with aluminum foil and spritz with the cooking spray.
3. In a bowl, combine all the ingredients, save for the corn. Stir with a whisk until well combined.
4. Coat the corn in the batter and put inside the basket.
5. Close the hood and AIR CRISP for 8 minutes until a golden brown color is achieved.
6. Serve hot.

Balsamic Mushroom Sliders With Pesto

Servings: 4
Cooking Time: 8 Minutes
Ingredients:

- 8 small portobello mushrooms, trimmed with gills removed
- 2 tablespoons canola oil
- 2 tablespoons balsamic vinegar
- 8 slider buns
- 1 tomato, sliced
- ½ cup pesto
- ½ cup micro greens

Directions:

1. Insert the Grill Grate and close the hood. Select GRILL, set the temperature to HIGH, and set the time to 8 minutes. Select START/STOP to begin preheating.
2. While the unit is preheating, brush the mushrooms with the oil and balsamic vinegar.
3. When the unit beeps to signify it has preheated, place the mushrooms, gill-side down, on the Grill Grate. Close the hood and GRILL for 8 minutes until the mushrooms are tender.
4. When cooking is complete, remove the mushrooms from the grill, and layer on the buns with tomato, pesto, and micro greens.

Roasted Lemony Broccoli

Servings: 6
Cooking Time: 15 Minutes
Ingredients:

- 2 heads broccoli, cut into florets
- 2 teaspoons extra-virgin olive oil, plus more for coating
- 1 teaspoon salt
- ½ teaspoon black pepper
- 1 clove garlic, minced
- ½ teaspoon lemon juice

Directions:

1. Cover the Crisper Basket with aluminum foil and coat with a light brushing of oil.
2. Insert the Crisper Basket and close the hood. Select ROAST, set the temperature to 375°F, and set the time to 15 minutes. Select START/STOP to begin preheating.
3. In a bowl, combine all ingredients, save for the lemon juice, and transfer to the Crisper Basket. Close the hood and ROAST for 15 minutes.
4. Serve with the lemon juice.

Mozzarella Broccoli Calzones

Servings: 4
Cooking Time: 24 Minutes
Ingredients:

- 1 head broccoli, trimmed into florets
- 2 tablespoons extra-virgin olive oil
- 1 store-bought pizza dough
- 2 to 3 tablespoons all-purpose flour, plus more for dusting
- 1 egg, beaten
- 2 cups shredded Mozzarella cheese
- 1 cup ricotta cheese
- ½ cup grated Parmesan cheese
- 1 garlic clove, grated
- Grated zest of 1 lemon
- ½ teaspoon red pepper flakes
- Cooking oil spray

Directions:
1. Insert the Crisper Basket and close the hood. Select AIR CRISP, set the temperature to 390°F, and set the time to 12 minutes. Select START/STOP to begin preheating.
2. Meanwhile, in a large bowl, toss the broccoli and olive oil until evenly coated.
3. When the unit beeps to signify it has preheated, add the broccoli to the basket. Close the hood and AIR CRISP for 6 minutes.
4. While the broccoli is cooking, divide the pizza dough into four equal pieces. Dust a clean work surface with the flour. Place the dough on the floured surface and roll each piece into an 8-inch round of even thickness. Dust your rolling pin and work surface with additional flour, as needed, to ensure the dough does not stick. Brush a thin coating of egg wash around the edges of each round.
5. After 6 minutes, shake the basket of broccoli. Place the basket back in the unit and close the hood to resume cooking.
6. Meanwhile, in a medium bowl, combine the Mozzarella, ricotta, Parmesan cheese, garlic, lemon zest, and red pepper flakes.
7. After cooking is complete, add the broccoli to the cheese mixture. Spoon one-quarter of the mixture onto one side of each dough. Fold the other half over the filling, and press firmly to seal the edges together. Brush each calzone all over with the remaining egg wash.
8. Select AIR CRISP, set the temperature to 390°F, and set the time to 12 minutes. Select START/STOP to begin preheating.
9. When the unit beeps to signify it has preheated, coat the Crisper Basket with cooking spray and place the calzones in the basket. AIR CRISP for 10 to 12 minutes, until golden brown.

Cheesy Broccoli Gratin

Servings: 2
Cooking Time: 12 To 14 Minutes
Ingredients:

- ⅓ cup fat-free milk
- 1 tablespoon all-purpose or gluten-free flour
- ½ tablespoon olive oil
- ½ teaspoon ground sage
- ¼ teaspoon kosher salt
- ⅛ teaspoon freshly ground black pepper
- 2 cups roughly chopped broccoli florets
- 6 tablespoons shredded Cheddar cheese
- 2 tablespoons panko bread crumbs
- 1 tablespoon grated Parmesan cheese
- Olive oil spray

Directions:
1. Select BAKE, set the temperature to 330°F, and set the time to 14 minutes. Select START/STOP to begin preheating.
2. Spritz a baking pan with olive oil spray.
3. Mix the milk, flour, olive oil, sage, salt, and pepper in a medium bowl and whisk to combine. Stir in the broccoli florets, Cheddar cheese, bread crumbs, and Parmesan cheese and toss to coat.
4. Pour the broccoli mixture into the prepared baking pan. Place the pan directly in the pot.
5. Close the hood and BAKE for 12 to 14 minutes until the top is golden brown and the broccoli is tender.
6. Serve immediately.

Veggie Taco Pie

Servings: 4

Cooking Time: 15 Minutes

Ingredients:

- 1 (15-ounce) can pinto beans, drained and rinsed
- 1 tablespoon chili powder
- 2 teaspoons ground cumin
- 2 teaspoons sea salt
- 1 teaspoon paprika
- ½ teaspoon garlic powder
- ½ teaspoon onion powder
- ½ teaspoon dried oregano
- 4 small flour tortillas
- 1 cup sour cream
- 1 (14-ounce) can diced tomatoes, drained
- 1 (15-ounce) can black beans, drained and rinsed
- 2 cups shredded cheddar cheese

Directions:

1. Insert the Cooking Pot and close the hood. Select BAKE, set the temperature to 350°F, and set the time to 15 minutes. Select START/STOP to begin preheating.

2. While the unit is preheating, in a large bowl, mash the pinto beans with a fork. Add the chili powder, cumin, salt, paprika, garlic powder, onion powder, and oregano and mix until well combined. Place a tortilla in the bottom of a 6-inch springform pan. Spread a quarter of the mashed pinto beans on the tortilla in an even layer, then layer on a quarter each of the sour cream, tomatoes, black beans, and cheddar cheese in that order. Repeat the layers three more times, ending with cheese.

3. When the unit beeps to signify it has preheated, place the pan in the Cooking Pot. Close the hood and cook for 15 minutes.

4. When cooking is complete, the cheese will be melted. Remove the pan from the grill and serve.

Sriracha Golden Cauliflower

Servings: 4

Cooking Time: 17 Minutes

Ingredients:

- ¼ cup vegan butter, melted
- ¼ cup sriracha sauce
- 4 cups cauliflower florets
- 1 cup bread crumbs
- 1 teaspoon salt

Directions:

1. Insert the Crisper Basket and close the hood. Select AIR CRISP, set the temperature to 375°F, and set the time to 17 minutes. Select START/STOP to begin preheating.

2. Mix the sriracha and vegan butter in a bowl and pour this mixture over the cauliflower, taking care to cover each floret entirely.

3. In a separate bowl, combine the bread crumbs and salt.

4. Dip the cauliflower florets in the bread crumbs, coating each one well. Transfer to the basket. Close the hood and AIR CRISP for 17 minutes.

5. Serve hot.

Simple Pesto Gnocchi

Servings: 4
Cooking Time: 15 Minutes

Ingredients:

- 1 package gnocchi
- 1 medium onion, chopped
- 3 cloves garlic, minced
-
- 1 tablespoon extra-virgin olive oil
- 1 jar pesto
- ⅓ cup grated Parmesan cheese

Directions:

1. Insert the Crisper Basket and close the hood. Select AIR CRISP, set the temperature to 340°F, and set the time to 15 minutes. Select START/STOP to begin preheating.
2. In a large bowl combine the onion, garlic, and gnocchi, and drizzle with the olive oil. Mix thoroughly.
3. Transfer the mixture to the basket. Close the hood and AIR CRISP for 15 minutes, stirring occasionally, making sure the gnocchi become light brown and crispy.
4. Add the pesto and Parmesan cheese, and give everything a good stir before serving.

Grilled Artichokes With Garlic Aioli

Servings: 4
Cooking Time: 33 Minutes

Ingredients:

- For the artichokes
- 4 artichokes
- 8 tablespoons avocado oil
- 8 tablespoons minced garlic
- Salt
- Freshly ground black pepper
- For the garlic aioli
- ½ cup mayonnaise
- 1 garlic clove, minced
- 1 tablespoon apple cider vinegar
- ⅛ teaspoon paprika

Directions:

1. Pull off the tough outer leaves near the stem of the artichoke and trim the bottom of the stem. Cut off the top third (½ to 1 inch) of the artichoke. Trim the tips of the leaves that surround the artichoke, as they can be sharp and thorny. Then cut the artichoke in half lengthwise. This exposes the artichoke heart. Use a spoon to remove the fuzzy choke, scraping to make sure it is cleaned away, then rinse the artichoke.
2. Insert the Grill Grate and close the hood. Select GRILL, set the temperature to LO, and set the time to 25 minutes. Select START/STOP to begin preheating.
3. While the unit is preheating, prepare 8 large pieces of aluminum foil for wrapping. Place an artichoke half, cut-side up, in the center of a foil piece. Drizzle 1 tablespoon of avocado oil into the center of the artichoke half and add 1 tablespoon of minced garlic. Season with salt and pepper. Seal the foil packet, making sure all sides are closed. Repeat for each artichoke half.
4. When the unit beeps to signify it has preheated, place the foil-wrapped artichokes on the Grill Grate. Close the hood and grill for 25 minutes.
5. When cooking is complete, the stem and heart will be soft, about the consistency of a cooked potato. Remove the artichokes from the foil.
6. Select GRILL, set the temperature to MAX, and set the time to 8 minutes. Place the artichokes on the Grill Grate, cut-side down. Select START/STOP and then press the PREHEAT button to skip preheating. Close the hood and cook for 4 minutes.
7. After 4 minutes, open the hood and flip the artichokes. Season with additional salt and pepper, if desired. Close the hood and cook for 4 minutes more.
8. When cooking is complete, remove the artichokes from the grill.
9. In a small bowl, combine the mayonnaise, garlic, vinegar, and paprika. Serve alongside the artichokes for dipping.

Vegetarian Meatballs

Servings: 3
Cooking Time: 18 Minutes
Ingredients:

- ½ cup grated carrots
- ½ cup sweet onions
- 2 tablespoons olive oil
- 1 cup rolled oats
- ½ cup roasted cashews
- 2 cups cooked chickpeas
- Juice of 1 lemon
- 2 tablespoons soy sauce
- 1 tablespoon flax meal
- 1 teaspoon garlic powder
- 1 teaspoon cumin
- ½ teaspoon turmeric

Directions:

1. Select ROAST, set the temperature to 350°F, and set the time to 6 minutes. Select START/STOP to begin preheating.
2. Mix together the carrots, onions, and olive oil in the pot and stir to combine.
3. Close the hood and ROAST for 6 minutes.
4. Meanwhile, put the oats and cashews in a food processor or blender and pulse until coarsely ground. Transfer the mixture to a large bowl. Add the chickpeas, lemon juice, and soy sauce to the food processor and pulse until smooth. Transfer the chickpea mixture to the bowl of oat and cashew mixture.
5. Remove the carrots and onions from the pot to the bowl of chickpea mixture. Add the flax meal, garlic powder, cumin, and turmeric and stir to incorporate.
6. Scoop tablespoon-sized portions of the veggie mixture and roll them into balls with your hands. Transfer the balls to the Crisper Basket in a single layer.
7. Increase the temperature to 370°F and BAKE for 12 minutes until golden through. Flip the balls halfway through the cooking time.
8. Serve warm.

Sweet Pepper Poppers

Servings: 4
Cooking Time: 7 Minutes
Ingredients:

- 10 mini sweet peppers
- ½ cup mayonnaise
- 1 cup shredded sharp cheddar cheese
- ½ teaspoon onion powder
- ⅛ teaspoon cayenne powder (optional)

Directions:

1. Insert the Grill Grate and close the hood. Select GRILL, set the temperature to HI, and set the time to 7 minutes. Select START/STOP to begin preheating.
2. While the unit is preheating, cut the peppers in half lengthwise and scoop out the seeds and membranes. In a small bowl, combine the mayonnaise, cheddar cheese, onion powder, and cayenne powder (if using). Spoon the cheese mixture into each sweet pepper half.
3. When the unit beeps to signify it has preheated, place the sweet peppers on the Grill Grate, cut-side up. Close the hood and grill for 7 minutes.
4. When cooking is complete, remove the peppers from the grill and serve. Or if you prefer your peppers more charred, continue cooking to your liking.

Vegetable And Cheese Stuffed Tomatoes

Servings: 4
Cooking Time: 16 To 20 Minutes
Ingredients:

- 4 medium beefsteak tomatoes, rinsed
- ½ cup grated carrot
- 1 medium onion, chopped
- 1 garlic clove, minced
- 2 teaspoons olive oil
- 2 cups fresh baby spinach
- ¼ cup crumbled low-sodium feta cheese
- ½ teaspoon dried basil

Directions:
1. Select BAKE, set the temperature to 350°F, and set the time to 20 minutes. Select START/STOP to begin preheating.
2. On your cutting board, cut a thin slice off the top of each tomato. Scoop out a ¼- to ½-inch-thick tomato pulp and place the tomatoes upside down on paper towels to drain. Set aside.
3. Stir together the carrot, onion, garlic, and olive oil in a baking pan. Place the pan directly in the pot. Close the hood and BAKE for 4 to 6 minutes, or until the carrot is crisp-tender.
4. Remove the pan from the grill and stir in the spinach, feta cheese, and basil.
5. Spoon ¼ of the vegetable mixture into each tomato and transfer the stuffed tomatoes to the pan.
6. Place the pan directly in the pot. Close the hood and BAKE for 12 to 14 minutes, or until the filling is hot and the tomatoes are lightly caramelized.
7. Let the tomatoes cool for 5 minutes and serve.

Sesame-thyme Whole Maitake Mushrooms

Servings: 2
Cooking Time: 15 Minutes
Ingredients:

- 1 tablespoon soy sauce
- 2 teaspoons toasted sesame oil
- 3 teaspoons vegetable oil, divided
- 1 garlic clove, minced
- 7 ounces maitake (hen of the woods) mushrooms
- ½ teaspoon flaky sea salt
- ½ teaspoon sesame seeds
- ½ teaspoon finely chopped fresh thyme leaves

Directions:
1. Insert the Crisper Basket and close the hood. Select ROAST, set the temperature to 300°F, and set the time to 15 minutes. Select START/STOP to begin preheating.
2. Whisk together the soy sauce, sesame oil, 1 teaspoon of vegetable oil, and garlic in a small bowl.
3. Arrange the mushrooms in the Crisper Basket in a single layer. Drizzle the soy sauce mixture over the mushrooms. Close the hood and ROAST for 10 minutes.
4. Flip the mushrooms and sprinkle the sea salt, sesame seeds, and thyme leaves on top. Drizzle the remaining 2 teaspoons of vegetable oil all over. Roast for an additional 5 minutes.
5. Remove the mushrooms from the basket to a plate and serve hot.

Crusted Brussels Sprouts With Sage

Servings: 4
Cooking Time: 15 Minutes
Ingredients:

- 1 pound Brussels sprouts, halved
- 1 cup bread crumbs
- 2 tablespoons grated Grana Padano cheese
- 1 tablespoon paprika
- 2 tablespoons canola oil
- 1 tablespoon chopped sage

Directions:
1. Line the Crisper Basket with parchment paper.
2. Insert the Crisper Basket and close the hood. Select ROAST, set the temperature to 400°F, and set the time to 15 minutes. Select START/STOP to begin preheating.
3. In a small bowl, thoroughly mix the bread crumbs, cheese, and paprika. In a large bowl, place the Brussels sprouts and drizzle the canola oil over the top. Sprinkle with the bread crumb mixture and toss to coat.
4. Place the Brussels sprouts in the Crisper Basket. Close the hood and ROAST for 15 minutes, or until the Brussels sprouts are lightly browned and crisp. Shake the basket a few times during cooking to ensure even cooking.
5. Transfer the Brussels sprouts to a plate and sprinkle the sage on top before serving.

Beef Stuffed Bell Peppers

Servings: 4
Cooking Time: 30 Minutes
Ingredients:

- 1 pound ground beef
- 1 tablespoon taco seasoning mix
- 1 can diced tomatoes and green chilis
- 4 green bell peppers
- 1 cup shredded Monterey jack cheese, divided

Directions:

1. Insert the Crisper Basket and close the hood. Select AIR CRISP, set the temperature to 350°F, and set the time to 15 minutes. Select START/STOP to begin preheating.

2. Set a skillet over a high heat and cook the ground beef for 8 minutes. Make sure it is cooked through and browned all over. Drain the fat.

3. Stir in the taco seasoning mix, and the diced tomatoes and green chilis. Allow the mixture to cook for a further 4 minutes.

4. In the meantime, slice the tops off the green peppers and remove the seeds and membranes.

5. When the meat mixture is fully cooked, spoon equal amounts of it into the peppers and top with the Monterey jack cheese. Then place the peppers into the basket. Close the hood and AIR CRISP for 15 minutes.

6. The peppers are ready when they are soft, and the cheese is bubbling and brown. Serve warm.

Grilled Vegetable Quesadillas

Servings: 4
Cooking Time: 8 Minutes
Ingredients:

- 1 medium onion, chopped
- 1 medium summer squash, halved lengthwise and thinly sliced into half-moons
- 1 medium zucchini, halved lengthwise and thinly sliced into half-moons
- Extra-virgin olive oil
- 4 (10-inch) flour tortillas
- 1 cup shredded mozzarella cheese
- ¼ cup chopped fresh cilantro (optional)

Directions:

1. Insert the Grill Grate and close the hood. Select GRILL, set the temperature to HI, and set the time to 8 minutes. Select START/STOP to begin preheating.

2. In a large bowl, combine the onion, summer squash, and zucchini and lightly coat with olive oil.

3. When the unit beeps to signify it has preheated, place the vegetables on the Grill Grate in a single layer. Close the hood and cook for 4 minutes.

4. While the vegetables are grilling, place the tortillas on a large tray and cover half of each with about ¼ cup of mozzarella.

5. After 4 minutes, open the hood and transfer the vegetables to the tortillas, evenly spreading on top of the cheese. Top the vegetables with the cilantro (if using). Fold the other half of each tortilla over to close. Place the quesadillas on the Grill Grate. Close the hood and cook for 2 minutes.

6. After 2 minutes, open the hood and flip the quesadillas. Close the hood and cook for 2 minutes more.

7. When cooking is complete, the cheese will be melted and the tortillas will be crispy. Remove the quesadillas from the grill and serve.

Sides, Snacks & Appetizers Recipes

Cheesy Apple Roll-ups

Servings:8
Cooking Time: 4 To 5 Minutes
Ingredients:

- 8 slices whole wheat sandwich bread
- 4 ounces Colby Jack cheese, grated
- ½ small apple, chopped
- 2 tablespoons butter, melted

Directions:

1. Insert the Crisper Basket and close the hood. Select AIR CRISP, set the temperature to 390°F, and set the time to 5 minutes. Select START/STOP to begin preheating.

2. Remove the crusts from the bread and flatten the slices with a rolling pin. Don't be gentle. Press hard so that bread will be very thin.

3. Top bread slices with cheese and chopped apple, dividing the ingredients evenly.

4. Roll up each slice tightly and secure each with one or two toothpicks.

5. Brush outside of rolls with melted butter.

6. Place in the Crisper Basket. Close the hood and AIR CRISP for 4 to 5 minutes, or until outside is crisp and nicely browned.

7. Serve hot.

Avocado Egg Rolls

Servings: 4
Cooking Time: 10 Minutes
Ingredients:

- 4 avocados, pitted and diced
- ½ white onion, diced
- ⅓ cup sun-dried tomatoes, chopped
- 1 (16-ounce) package egg roll wrappers (about 20 wrappers)
- ¼ cup water, for sealing
- 4 tablespoons avocado oil

Directions:

1. Insert the Grill Grate and close the hood. Select GRILL, set the temperature to LO, and set the time to 10 minutes. Select START/STOP to begin preheating.

2. While the unit is preheating, place the diced avocado in a large bowl. Add the onion and sun-dried tomatoes and gently fold together, being careful to not mash the avocado.

3. Place an egg roll wrapper on a flat surface with a corner facing you (like a diamond). Add 2 to 3 tablespoons of the filling in the center of the wrapper. The amount should be about 2½ inches wide. Gently lift the bottom corner of the wrapper over the filling, fold in the sides, and roll away from you to close. Dip your finger into the water and run it over the top corner of the wrapper to seal it. Continue filling, folding, and sealing the rest of the egg rolls.

4. When the unit beeps to signify it has preheated, brush the avocado oil on all sides of the egg rolls. Place the egg rolls on the Grill Grate, seam-side down. Close the hood and grill for 5 minutes.

5. After 5 minutes, open the hood and flip the egg rolls. Give them another brush of avocado oil. Close the hood and cook for 5 minutes more.

6. When cooking is complete, the wrappers will be golden brown. Remove from the grill and serve.

Cayenne Sesame Nut Mix

Servings:4
Cooking Time: 2 Minutes
Ingredients:

- 1 tablespoon buttery spread, melted
- 2 teaspoons honey
- ¼ teaspoon cayenne pepper
- 2 teaspoons sesame seeds
- ¼ teaspoon kosher salt
- ¼ teaspoon freshly ground black pepper
- 1 cup cashews
- 1 cup almonds
- 1 cup mini pretzels
- 1 cup rice squares cereal
- Cooking spray

Directions:

1. Select BAKE, set the temperature to 360°F, and set the time to 2 minutes. Select START/STOP to begin preheating.

2. In a large bowl, combine the buttery spread, honey, cayenne pepper, sesame seeds, kosher salt, and black pepper, then add the cashews, almonds, pretzels, and rice squares, tossing to coat.

3. Spray a baking pan with cooking spray, then pour the mixture into the pan. Place the pan directly in the pot. Close the hood and BAKE for 2 minutes.

4. Remove the sesame mix from the grill and allow to cool in the pan on a wire rack for 5 minutes before serving.

Maple Butter Corn Bread

Servings: 4
Cooking Time: 40 Minutes
Ingredients:

- For the corn bread
- 1 cup all-purpose flour
- 1 cup yellow cornmeal
- 2 teaspoons baking powder
- 1 teaspoon salt
- 1¼ cups milk
- ⅓ cup canola oil
- 1 large egg
- 1 (14.75-ounce) can cream-style sweet corn
- Cooking spray
- For the maple butter
- 1 tablespoon light brown sugar, packed
- 1 tablespoon milk
- 8 tablespoons (1 stick) unsalted butter, at room temperature
- 1 tablespoon maple syrup

Directions:

1. Insert the Cooking Pot and close the hood. Select BAKE, set the temperature to 350°F, and set the time to 40 minutes. Select START/STOP to begin preheating.

2. While the unit is preheating, in a large bowl, combine the flour, cornmeal, baking powder, salt, milk, oil, egg, and sweet corn. Mix until just combined. Grease a 9-by-5-inch loaf pan with cooking spray and pour in the corn bread batter.

3. When the unit beeps to signify it has preheated, place the pan in the Cooking Pot. Close the hood and cook for 40 minutes. If using a metal loaf pan, check the corn bread after 30 minutes, as metal pans may cook faster than glass. Bake until golden brown and the mix is completely baked through.

4. When cooking is complete, the corn bread should be golden brown and a toothpick inserted into the center of the corn bread comes out clean. Remove the pan from the grill and set aside to cool.

5. In a small bowl, whisk together the brown sugar and milk until the sugar is dissolved. Add the butter and continue whisking. Add the maple syrup and continue whisking until fully combined.

6. Cut the corn bread into slices, top with the butter, and serve.

Breaded Green Olives

Servings: 4
Cooking Time: 8 Minutes
Ingredients:
- 1 jar pitted green olives
- ½ cup all-purpose flour
- Salt and pepper, to taste
- ½ cup bread crumbs
- 1 egg
- Cooking spray

Directions:
1. Insert the Crisper Basket and close the hood. Select AIR CRISP, set the temperature to 400°F, and set the time to 8 minutes. Select START/STOP to begin preheating.
2. Remove the olives from the jar and dry thoroughly with paper towels.
3. In a small bowl, combine the flour with salt and pepper to taste. Place the bread crumbs in another small bowl. In a third small bowl, beat the egg.
4. Spritz the Crisper Basket with cooking spray.
5. Dip the olives in the flour, then the egg, and then the bread crumbs.
6. Place the breaded olives in the basket. It is okay to stack them. Spray the olives with cooking spray. Close the hood and AIR CRISP for 6 minutes. Flip the olives and AIR CRISP for an additional 2 minutes, or until brown and crisp.
7. Cool before serving.

Goat Cheese Bruschetta With Tomatoes

Servings: 4
Cooking Time: 8 Minutes
Ingredients:
- 8 ounces cherry tomatoes (about 35)
- 8 fresh basil leaves
- 1 tablespoon balsamic vinegar
- 1 (8-ounce) baguette
- ½ cup extra-virgin olive oil
- 2 tablespoons garlic powder
- 8 ounces goat cheese (unflavored)

Directions:
1. Insert the Grill Grate and close the hood. Select GRILL, set the temperature to HI, and set the time to 8 minutes. Select START/STOP to begin preheating.
2. While the unit is preheating, quarter the cherry tomatoes. Slice the basil leaves into very thin ribbons. Place the tomatoes and basil in a medium bowl. Add the balsamic vinegar and toss to coat.
3. Slice the baguette into ½-inch slices. In a small bowl, whisk together the olive oil and garlic powder. Brush both sides of the baguette slices with the olive oil mixture.
4. When the unit beeps to signify it has preheated, place half the baguette slices on the Grill Grate in a single layer. Close the hood and cook for 4 minutes. After 4 minutes, remove the baguettes from the grill and set aside on a plate. Place the remaining slices on the Grill Grate. Close the hood and cook for 4 minutes.
5. When cooking is complete, spread a layer of goat cheese on the baguette slices. Top with the tomato-basil mixture and serve.

Homemade Bbq Chicken Pizza

Servings: 1
Cooking Time: 8 Minutes
Ingredients:
- 1 piece naan bread
- ¼ cup Barbecue sauce
- ¼ cup shredded Monterrey Jack cheese
- ¼ cup shredded Mozzarella cheese
- ½ chicken herby sausage, sliced
- 2 tablespoons red onion, thinly sliced
- Chopped cilantro or parsley, for garnish
- Cooking spray

Directions:
1. Insert the Crisper Basket and close the hood. Select AIR CRISP, set the temperature to 400°F, and set the time to 8 minutes. Select START/STOP to begin preheating.
2. Spritz the bottom of naan bread with cooking spray, then transfer to the Crisper Basket.
3. Brush with the Barbecue sauce. Top with the cheeses, sausage, and finish with the red onion.
4. Close the hood and AIR CRISP for 8 minutes until the cheese is melted.
5. Garnish with the chopped cilantro or parsley before slicing to serve.

Cheesy Steak Fries

Servings: 5
Cooking Time: 20 Minutes
Ingredients:

- 1 bag frozen steak fries
- Cooking spray
- Salt and pepper, to taste
- ½ cup beef gravy
- 1 cup shredded Mozzarella cheese
- 2 scallions, green parts only, chopped

Directions:

1. Insert the Crisper Basket and close the hood. Select AIR CRISP, set the temperature to 400°F, and set the time to 20 minutes. Select START/STOP to begin preheating.
2. Place the frozen steak fries in the basket. Close the hood and AIR CRISP for 10 minutes. Shake the basket and spritz the fries with cooking spray. Sprinkle with salt and pepper. AIR CRISP for an additional 8 minutes.
3. Pour the beef gravy into a medium, microwave-safe bowl. Microwave for 30 seconds, or until the gravy is warm.
4. Sprinkle the fries with the cheese. Close the hood and AIR CRISP for an additional 2 minutes, until the cheese is melted.
5. Transfer the fries to a serving dish. Drizzle the fries with gravy and sprinkle the scallions on top for a green garnish. Serve.

French Fries

Servings: 4
Cooking Time: 25 Minutes
Ingredients:

- 1 pound russet or Idaho potatoes, cut in 2-inch strips
- 3 tablespoons canola oil

Directions:

1. Place the potatoes in a large bowl and cover them with cold water. Let soak for 30 minutes. Drain well, then pat with a paper towel until very dry.
2. Insert the Crisper Basket and close the hood. Select AIR CRISP, set the temperature to 390°F, and set the time to 25 minutes. Select START/STOP to begin preheating.
3. Meanwhile, in a large bowl, toss the potatoes with the oil.
4. When the unit beeps to signify it has preheated, add the potatoes to the basket. Close the hood and AIR CRISP for 10 minutes.
5. After 10 minutes, shake the basket well. Place the basket back in the unit and close the hood to resume cooking.
6. After 10 minutes, check for desired crispness. Continue cooking up to 5 minutes more, if necessary.
7. When cooking is complete, serve immediately with your favorite dipping sauce.

Sweet Potato Chips

Servings:1
Cooking Time: 8 To 10 Hours
Ingredients:

- 1 sweet potato, peeled
- ½ tablespoon avocado oil
- ½ teaspoon sea salt

Directions:

1. Using a mandoline, thinly slice (⅛ inch or less) the sweet potato.
2. In a large bowl, toss the sweet potato slices with the oil until evenly coated. Season with the salt.
3. Place the sweet potato slices flat on the Crisper Basket. Arrange them in a single layer, without any slices touching each another.
4. Place the basket in the pot and close the hood.
5. Select DEHYDRATE, set the temperature to 120°F, and set the time to 10 hours. Select START/STOP.
6. After 8 hours, check for desired doneness. Continue dehydrating for 2 more hours, if necessary.
7. When cooking is complete, remove the basket from the pot. Transfer the sweet potato chips to an airtight container and store at room temperature.

Mushroom And Spinach Calzones

Servings: 4
Cooking Time: 26 To 27 Minutes

Ingredients:

- 2 tablespoons olive oil
- 1 onion, chopped
- 2 garlic cloves, minced
- ¼ cup chopped mushrooms
- 1 pound spinach, chopped
- 1 tablespoon Italian seasoning
- ½ teaspoon oregano
- Salt and black pepper, to taste
- 1½ cups marinara sauce
- 1 cup ricotta cheese, crumbled
- 1 pizza crust
- Cooking spray

Directions:

1. Make the Filling:
2. Heat the olive oil in a pan over medium heat until shimmering.
3. Add the onion, garlic, and mushrooms and sauté for 4 minutes, or until softened.
4. Stir in the spinach and sauté for 2 to 3 minutes, or until the spinach is wilted. Sprinkle with the Italian seasoning, oregano, salt, and pepper and mix well.
5. Add the marinara sauce and cook for about 5 minutes, stirring occasionally, or until the sauce is thickened.
6. Remove the pan from the heat and stir in the ricotta cheese. Set aside.
7. Make the Calzones:
8. Spritz the Crisper Basket with cooking spray.
9. Insert the Crisper Basket and close the hood. Select AIR CRISP, set the temperature to 375ºF, and set the time to 15 minutes. Select START/STOP to begin preheating.
10. Roll the pizza crust out with a rolling pin on a lightly floured work surface, then cut it into 4 rectangles.
11. Spoon ¼ of the filling into each rectangle and fold in half. Crimp the edges with a fork to seal. Mist them with cooking spray.
12. Place the calzones in the Crisper Basket. Close the hood and AIR CRISP for 15 minutes, flipping once, or until the calzones are golden brown and crisp.
13. Transfer the calzones to a paper towel-lined plate and serve.

Balsamic Broccoli

Servings: 4
Cooking Time: 10 Minutes

Ingredients:

- 4 tablespoons soy sauce
- 4 tablespoons balsamic vinegar
- 2 tablespoons canola oil
- 2 teaspoons maple syrup
- 2 heads broccoli, trimmed into florets
- Red pepper flakes, for garnish
- Sesame seeds, for garnish

Directions:

1. Insert the Grill Grate and close the hood. Select GRILL, set the temperature to MAX, and set the time to 10 minutes. Select START/STOP to begin preheating.
2. While the unit is preheating, in a large bowl, whisk together the soy sauce, balsamic vinegar, oil, and maple syrup. Add the broccoli and toss to coat evenly.
3. When the unit beeps to signify it has preheated, place the broccoli on the Grill Grate. Close the hood and GRILL for 8 to 10 minutes, until charred on all sides.
4. When cooking is complete, place the broccoli on a large serving platter. Garnish with red pepper flakes and sesame seeds. Serve immediately.

Crispy Spiced Potatoes

Servings: 4
Cooking Time: 20 Minutes
Ingredients:

- 2 pounds baby red potatoes, quartered
- 2 tablespoons extra-virgin olive oil
- ¼ cup dried onion flakes
- 1 teaspoon dried rosemary
- ½ teaspoon onion powder
- ½ teaspoon garlic powder
- ¼ teaspoon celery powder
- ¼ teaspoon freshly ground black pepper
- ½ teaspoon dried parsley
- ½ teaspoon sea salt

Directions:

1. Insert the Crisper Basket and close the hood. Select AIR CRISP, set the temperature to 390°F, and set the time to 20 minutes. Select START/STOP to begin preheating.
2. Meanwhile, place all the ingredients in a large bowl and toss until evenly coated.
3. When the unit beeps to signify it has preheated, add the potatoes to the basket. Close the hood and AIR CRISP for 10 minutes.
4. After 10 minutes, shake the basket well. Place the basket back in the unit and close the hood to resume cooking.
5. After 10 minutes, check for desired crispness. Continue cooking up to 5 minutes more, if necessary.

Spicy Kale Chips

Servings: 4
Cooking Time: 8 To 12 Minutes
Ingredients:

- 5 cups kale, large stems removed and chopped
- 2 teaspoons canola oil
- ¼ teaspoon smoked paprika
- ¼ teaspoon kosher salt
- Cooking spray

Directions:

1. Insert the Crisper Basket and close the hood. Select AIR CRISP, set the temperature to 390°F, and set the time to 6 minutes. Select START/STOP to begin preheating.
2. In a large bowl, toss the kale, canola oil, smoked paprika, and kosher salt.
3. Spray the Crisper Basket with cooking spray, then place half the kale in the basket. Close the hood and AIR CRISP for 2 to 3 minutes.
4. Shake the basket and AIR CRISP for 2 to 3 more minutes, or until crispy. Repeat this process with the remaining kale.
5. Remove the kale and allow to cool on a wire rack for 3 to 5 minutes before serving.

Crispy Cod Fingers

Servings: 4
Cooking Time: 12 Minutes
Ingredients:

- 2 eggs
- 2 tablespoons milk
- 2 cups flour
- 1 cup cornmeal
- 1 teaspoon seafood seasoning
- Salt and black pepper, to taste
- 1 cup bread crumbs
- 1 pound cod fillets, cut into 1-inch strips

Directions:

1. Insert the Crisper Basket and close the hood. Select AIR CRISP, set the temperature to 400°F, and set the time to 12 minutes. Select START/STOP to begin preheating.
2. Beat the eggs with the milk in a shallow bowl. In another shallow bowl, combine the flour, cornmeal, seafood seasoning, salt, and pepper. On a plate, place the bread crumbs.
3. Dredge the cod strips, one at a time, in the flour mixture, then in the egg mixture, finally in the bread crumb to coat evenly.
4. Arrange the cod strips in the Crisper Basket. Close the hood and AIR CRISP for 12 minutes until crispy.
5. Transfer the cod strips to a paper towel-lined plate and serve warm.

Easy Muffuletta Sliders With Olives

Servings:8
Cooking Time: 5 To 7 Minutes
Ingredients:

- ¼ pound thinly sliced deli ham
- ¼ pound thinly sliced pastrami
- 4 ounces low-fat Mozzarella cheese, grated
- 8 slider buns, split in half
- Cooking spray
- 1 tablespoon sesame seeds
- Olive Mix:
- ½ cup sliced green olives with pimentos
- ¼ cup sliced black olives
- ¼ cup chopped kalamata olives
- 1 teaspoon red wine vinegar
- ¼ teaspoon basil
- ⅛ teaspoon garlic powder

Directions:

1. Insert the Crisper Basket and close the hood. Select BAKE, set the temperature to 360ºF, and set the time to 7 minutes. Select START/STOP to begin preheating.
2. Combine all the ingredients for the olive mix in a small bowl and stir well.
3. Stir together the ham, pastrami, and cheese in a medium bowl and divide the mixture into 8 equal portions.
4. Assemble the sliders: Top each bottom bun with 1 portion of meat and cheese, 2 tablespoons of olive mix, finished by the remaining buns. Lightly spritz the tops with cooking spray. Scatter the sesame seeds on top.
5. Working in batches, arrange the sliders in the Crisper Basket. Close the hood and BAKE for 5 to 7 minutes until the cheese melts.
6. Transfer to a large plate and repeat with the remaining sliders.
7. Serve immediately.

One-pot Nachos

Servings: 4
Cooking Time: 10 Minutes
Ingredients:

- 1 pound ground beef
- 1 (1-ounce) packet taco seasoning mix
- 1 (16-ounce) can refried beans
- 1 (14.5-ounce) can diced tomatoes, drained
- 2 cups sour cream
- 3 cups shredded Mexican cheese blend
- 2 cups shredded iceberg lettuce
- 1 cup sliced black olives
- Sliced scallions, both white and green parts, for garnish
- 1 (10- to 13-ounce) bag tortilla chips

Directions:

1. Insert the Cooking Pot and close the hood. Select GRILL, set the temperature to MED, and set the time to 10 minutes. Select START/STOP to begin preheating.
2. When the unit beeps to signify it has preheated, place the ground beef in the Cooking Pot and sprinkle it with the taco seasoning. Using a wooden spoon or spatula, break apart the ground beef. Close the hood and cook for 5 minutes.
3. After 5 minutes, open the hood and stir the ground beef to mix a little more with the taco seasoning. Evenly spread the ground beef across the bottom of the pot. Add the refried beans in an even layer over the meat, then an even layer of the diced tomatoes. Close the hood and cook for 5 minutes more.
4. When cooking is complete, remove the Cooking Pot from the unit and place it on a heatproof surface. Add an even layer each of sour cream, shredded cheese, shredded lettuce, and olives on top. Garnish with scallions and serve with the tortilla chips.

Jalapeño Poppers

Servings: 4
Cooking Time: 10 Minutes
Ingredients:

- 8 jalapeños
- 4 ounces cream cheese, at room temperature
- ¼ cup grated Parmesan cheese
- ¼ cup shredded cheddar cheese
- ½ teaspoon garlic powder
- 8 slices thin-cut bacon

Directions:
1. Insert the Grill Grate and close the hood. Select GRILL, set the temperature to HI, and set the time to 10 minutes. Select START/STOP to begin preheating.
2. While the unit is preheating, slice the jalapeños in half lengthwise and scoop out the seeds and membranes.
3. In a small bowl, combine the cream cheese, Parmesan cheese, cheddar cheese, and garlic powder. Scoop the cheese mixture evenly into each jalapeño half.
4. Slice the bacon in half lengthwise so you have 16 strips. Wrap each jalapeño half with a bacon slice, starting from the bottom end and wrapping around until it reaches the top of the jalapeño.
5. When the unit beeps to signify it has preheated, place the jalapeños on the Grill Grate, filling-side up. Close the hood and grill for 10 minutes.
6. When cooking is complete, the bacon will be cooked and beginning to crisp. If you prefer your bacon crispier or charred, continue cooking to your liking. Remove the poppers from the grill and serve.

Brussels Sprouts And Bacon

Servings: 4
Cooking Time: 12 Minutes
Ingredients:

- 1 pound Brussels sprouts, trimmed and halved
- 2 tablespoons extra-virgin olive oil
- 1 teaspoon sea salt
- ½ teaspoon freshly ground black pepper
- 6 slices bacon, chopped

Directions:
1. Insert the Crisper Basket and close the hood. Select AIR CRISP, set the temperature to 390°F, and set the time to 12 minutes. Select START/STOP to begin preheating.
2. Meanwhile, in a large bowl, toss the Brussels sprouts with the olive oil, salt, pepper, and bacon.
3. When the unit beeps to signify it has preheated, add the Brussels sprouts to the basket. Close the hood and AIR CRISP for 10 minutes.
4. After 6 minutes, shake the basket of Brussels sprouts. Place the basket back in the unit and close the hood to resume cooking.
5. After 6 minutes, check for desired crispness. Continue cooking up to 2 more minutes, if necessary.

Mozzarella Sticks

Servings: 4
Cooking Time: 8 Minutes
Ingredients:

- 2 large eggs
- 2 cups plain bread crumbs
- 2 tablespoons Italian seasoning
- 10 to 12 mozzarella cheese sticks
- Marinara sauce, for dipping

Directions:
1. In a large bowl, whisk the eggs. In a separate large bowl, combine the bread crumbs and Italian seasoning.
2. Dip each cheese stick in the egg and then dip it in the bread crumbs to evenly coat. Place the breaded mozzarella sticks on a baking sheet or flat tray, then freeze for 30 minutes.
3. Insert the Grill Grate and close the hood. Select GRILL, set the temperature to MED, and set the time to 8 minutes. Select START/STOP to begin preheating.
4. When the unit beeps to signify it has preheated, open the hood and place the mozzarella sticks on the Grill Grate. Close the hood and grill for 8 minutes.
5. When cooking is complete, the mozzarella sticks will be golden brown and crispy. If you prefer browner mozzarella sticks, continue cooking to your liking. Serve with the marinara sauce on the side.

Cheese And Ham Stuffed Baby Bella

Servings: 8
Cooking Time: 12 Minutes
Ingredients:

- 4 ounces Mozzarella cheese, cut into pieces
- ½ cup diced ham
- 2 green onions, chopped
- 2 tablespoons bread crumbs
- ½ teaspoon garlic powder
- ¼ teaspoon ground oregano
- ¼ teaspoon ground black pepper
- 1 to 2 teaspoons olive oil
- 16 fresh Baby Bella mushrooms, stemmed removed

Directions:

1. Process the cheese, ham, green onions, bread crumbs, garlic powder, oregano, and pepper in a food processor until finely chopped.
2. With the food processor running, slowly drizzle in 1 to 2 teaspoons olive oil until a thick paste has formed. Transfer the mixture to a bowl.
3. Evenly divide the mixture into the mushroom caps and lightly press down the mixture.
4. Insert the Crisper Basket and close the hood. Select ROAST, set the temperature to 390°F, and set the time to 12 minutes. Select START/STOP to begin preheating.
5. Lay the mushrooms in the Crisper Basket in a single layer. You'll need to work in batches to avoid overcrowding.
6. Close the hood and ROAST for 12 minutes until the mushrooms are lightly browned and tender.
7. Remove from the basket to a plate and repeat with the remaining mushrooms.
8. Let the mushrooms cool for 5 minutes and serve warm.

Buttermilk Marinated Chicken Wings

Servings: 4
Cooking Time: 17 To 19 Minutes
Ingredients:

- 2 pounds chicken wings
- Marinade:
- 1 cup buttermilk
- ½ teaspoon salt
- ½ teaspoon black pepper
- Coating:
- 1 cup flour
- 1 cup panko bread crumbs
- 2 tablespoons poultry seasoning
- 2 teaspoons salt
- Cooking spray

Directions:

1. Whisk together all the ingredients for the marinade in a large bowl.
2. Add the chicken wings to the marinade and toss well. Transfer to the refrigerator to marinate for at least an hour.
3. Spritz the Crisper Basket with cooking spray.
4. Insert the Crisper Basket and close the hood. Select AIR CRISP, set the temperature to 360°F, and set the time to 19 minutes. Select START/STOP to begin preheating.
5. Thoroughly combine all the ingredients for the coating in a shallow bowl.
6. Remove the chicken wings from the marinade and shake off any excess. Roll them in the coating mixture.
7. Place the chicken wings in the Crisper Basket in a single layer. Mist the wings with cooking spray. You'll need to work in batches to avoid overcrowding.
8. Close the hood and AIR CRISP for 17 to 19 minutes, or until the wings are crisp and golden brown on the outside. Flip the wings halfway through the cooking time.
9. Remove from the basket to a plate and repeat with the remaining wings.
10. Serve hot.

Cheesy Garlic Bread

Servings: 4
Cooking Time: 8 Minutes

Ingredients:

- 1 loaf (about 1 pound) French bread
- 8 tablespoons (1 stick) unsalted butter, at room temperature
- 1 tablespoon minced garlic
- 1 teaspoon garlic powder
- 1½ cups shredded mozzarella cheese
- ½ cup shredded Colby Jack cheese
- 1 teaspoon dried parsley

Directions:

1. Insert the Grill Grate and close the hood. Select GRILL, set the temperature to MED, and set the time to 8 minutes. Select START/STOP to begin preheating.

2. While the unit is preheating, cut the French bread in half lengthwise. In a small bowl, mix together the butter, garlic, and garlic powder until well combined. Spread the garlic butter on both bread halves. Top each half with the mozzarella and Colby Jack cheeses. Sprinkle the dried parsley on top.

3. When the unit beeps to signify it has preheated, place the cheese-topped bread on the Grill Grate. Close the hood and grill for 8 minutes.

4. When cooking is complete, the cheese will be melted and golden brown. Remove the bread from the grill and serve.

Sweet Potato Fries With Honey-butter Sauce

Servings: 4
Cooking Time: 20 Minutes

Ingredients:

- For the sweet potato fries
- 2 medium sweet potatoes, cut into ¼-inch-thick slices
- 3 teaspoons avocado oil
- 1 teaspoon salt
- ½ teaspoon paprika
- ½ teaspoon garlic powder
- ¼ teaspoon freshly ground black pepper
- For the honey butter
- 1 tablespoon honey
- 1 teaspoon powdered sugar
- 8 tablespoons (1 stick) salted butter, at room temperature

Directions:

1. Insert the Crisper Basket and close the hood. Select AIR CRISP, set the temperature to 400°F, and set the time to 20 minutes. Select START/STOP to begin preheating.

2. In a large bowl, drizzle the sweet potatoes with the avocado oil and toss to coat. In a small bowl, mix together the salt, paprika, garlic powder, and pepper. Sprinkle the seasoning over the sweet potatoes and toss gently to coat.

3. When the unit beeps to signify it has preheated, place the sweet potato fries in the Crisper Basket. Close the hood and cook for 10 minutes.

4. After 10 minutes, open the hood and shake the basket. Close the hood and cook for 5 minutes more. Open the hood again and shake the basket. If the fries are to your desired crispness, then remove them. If not, close the hood and cook up to 5 minutes more.

5. In a small bowl, whisk together the honey and powdered sugar until the sugar is dissolved. Add the butter and continue whisking. Serve alongside the fries.

Grilled Carrots With Honey Glazed

Servings: 4
Cooking Time: 10 Minutes
Ingredients:

- 6 medium carrots, peeled and cut lengthwise
- 1 tablespoon canola oil
- 2 tablespoons unsalted butter, melted
- ¼ cup brown sugar, melted
- ¼ cup honey
- ⅛ teaspoon sea salt

Directions:

1. Insert the Grill Grate and close the hood. Select GRILL, set the temperature to MAX, and set the time to 10 minutes. Select START/STOP to begin preheating.
2. In a large bowl, toss the carrots and oil until well coated.
3. When the unit beeps to signify it has preheated, place carrots on the center of the Grill Grate. Close the hood and GRILL for 5 minutes.
4. Meanwhile, in a small bowl, whisk together the butter, brown sugar, honey, and salt.
5. After 5 minutes, open the hood and baste the carrots with the glaze. Using tongs, turn the carrots and baste the other side. Close the hood and GRILL for another 5 minutes.
6. When cooking is complete, serve immediately.

Sauces, Dips, And Dressings Recipes

Lemon Dijon Vinaigrette

Servings:6
Cooking Time: 0 Minutes
Ingredients:

- ¼ cup extra-virgin olive oil
- 1 garlic clove, minced
- 2 tablespoons freshly squeezed lemon juice
- 1 teaspoon Dijon mustard
- ½ teaspoon raw honey
- ¼ teaspoon salt
- ¼ teaspoon dried basil

Directions:

1. Place all the ingredients in a mason jar. Cover and shake vigorously until thoroughly mixed and well emulsified.
2. Serve chilled.

Garlic Lime Tahini Dressing

Servings:1
Cooking Time: 0 Minutes
Ingredients:

- ⅓ cup tahini
- 3 tablespoons filtered water
- 2 tablespoons freshly squeezed lime juice
- 1 tablespoon apple cider vinegar
- 1 teaspoon lime zest
- 1½ teaspoons raw honey
- ¼ teaspoon garlic powder
- ¼ teaspoon salt

Directions:

1. Whisk together the tahini, water, vinegar, lime juice, lime zest, honey, salt, and garlic powder in a small bowl until well emulsified.
2. Serve immediately, or refrigerate in an airtight container for to 1 week.

Balsamic Dressing

Servings:1
Cooking Time: 0 Minutes
Ingredients:

- 2 tablespoons Dijon mustard
- ¼ cup balsamic vinegar
- ¾ cup olive oil

Directions:

1. Put all ingredients in a jar with a tight-fitting lid. Put on the lid and shake vigorously until thoroughly combined. Refrigerate until ready to use and shake well before serving.

Pico De Gallo

Servings: 2
Cooking Time: 0 Minutes
Ingredients:

- 3 large tomatoes, chopped
- ½ small red onion, diced
- ⅛ cup chopped fresh cilantro
- 3 garlic cloves, chopped
- 2 tablespoons chopped pickled jalapeño pepper
- 1 tablespoon lime juice
- ¼ teaspoon pink Himalayan salt (optional)

Directions:

1. In a medium bowl, combine all the ingredients and mix with a wooden spoon.

Meats Recipes

Pork Spareribs With Peanut Sauce

Servings: 6
Cooking Time: 30 Minutes
Ingredients:

- 2 (2- to 3-pound) racks St. Louis–style spareribs
- Sea salt
- ½ cup crunchy peanut butter
- 1 tablespoon rice vinegar
- 2 tablespoons hoisin sauce
- 1 tablespoon honey
- 2 tablespoons soy sauce
- 1 teaspoon garlic powder

Directions:

1. Plug the thermometer into the unit. Insert the Grill Grate and close the hood. Select GRILL, set the temperature to MED, and select PRESET. Use the arrows to the right to select PORK. The unit will default to WELL to cook the pork to a safe temperature. Insert the Smart Thermometer into the thickest part of the meat between two bones, making sure it does not touch bone. Select START/STOP to begin preheating.
2. When the unit beeps to signify it has preheated, place the racks of ribs on the Grill Grate. Close the hood to begin cooking.
3. When the Foodi™ Grill indicates it's time to flip, open the hood and flip the racks. Then close the hood to continue cooking.
4. While the ribs are cooking, in a small bowl, combine the peanut butter, vinegar, hoisin sauce, honey, soy sauce, and garlic powder and mix until well blended.
5. When cooking is complete, the Smart Thermometer will indicate that the desired internal temperature has been reached. Open the hood and remove the ribs. Either pour the sauce over the ribs or divide the sauce between individual bowls for dipping. Serve.

Pork Sausage With Cauliflower Mash

Servings: 6
Cooking Time: 27 Minutes
Ingredients:

- 1 pound cauliflower, chopped
- 6 pork sausages, chopped
- ½ onion, sliced
- 3 eggs, beaten
- ⅓ cup Colby cheese
- 1 teaspoon cumin powder
- ½ teaspoon tarragon
- ½ teaspoon sea salt
- ½ teaspoon ground black pepper
- Cooking spray

Directions:

1. Select BAKE, set the temperature to 365°F, and set the time to 27 minutes. Select START/STOP to begin preheating.

2. Spritz a baking pan with cooking spray.

3. In a saucepan over medium heat, boil the cauliflower until tender. Place the boiled cauliflower in a food processor and pulse until puréed. Transfer to a large bowl and combine with remaining ingredients until well blended.

4. Pour the cauliflower and sausage mixture into the baking pan. Place the pan directly in the pot. Close the hood and BAKE for 27 minutes, or until lightly browned.

5. Divide the mixture among six serving dishes and serve warm.

Cheesy Jalapeño Popper Burgers

Servings: 4
Cooking Time: 9 Minutes
Ingredients:

- 2 jalapeño peppers, seeded, stemmed, and minced
- ½ cup shredded Cheddar cheese
- 4 ounces cream cheese, at room temperature
- 4 slices bacon, cooked and crumbled
- 2 pounds ground beef
- ½ teaspoon chili powder
- ¼ teaspoon paprika
- ¼ teaspoon freshly ground black pepper
- 4 hamburger buns
- 4 slices pepper Jack cheese
- Lettuce, sliced tomato, and sliced red onion, for topping (optional)

Directions:

1. Insert the Grill Grate and close the hood. Select GRILL, set the temperature to HIGH, and set the time to 9 minutes. Select START/STOP to begin preheating.

2. In a medium bowl, combine the peppers, Cheddar cheese, cream cheese, and bacon until well combined.

3. Form the ground beef into 8¼-inch-thick patties. Spoon some of the filling mixture onto four of the patties, then place a second patty on top of each to make four burgers. Use your fingers to pinch the edges of the patties together to seal in the filling. Reshape the patties with your hands as needed.

4. Combine the chili powder, paprika, and pepper in a small bowl. Sprinkle the mixture onto both sides of the burgers.

5. When the units beeps to signify it has preheated, place the burgers on the Grill Grate. Close the hood and GRILL for 4 minutes without flipping. Cooking is complete when the internal temperature of the beef reaches at least 145°F on a food thermometer. If needed, GRILL for up to 5 more minutes.

6. Place the burgers on the hamburger buns and top with pepper Jack cheese. Add lettuce, tomato, and red onion, if desired.

Potato And Prosciutto Salad

Servings: 8
Cooking Time: 7 Minutes
Ingredients:

- Salad:
- 4 pounds potatoes, boiled and cubed
- 15 slices prosciutto, diced
- 2 cups shredded Cheddar cheese
- Dressing:
- 15 ounces sour cream
- 2 tablespoons mayonnaise
- 1 teaspoon salt
- 1 teaspoon black pepper
- 1 teaspoon dried basil

Directions:
1. Select AIR CRISP, set the temperature to 350°F, and set the time to 7 minutes. Select START/STOP to begin preheating.
2. Put the potatoes, prosciutto, and Cheddar in a baking pan. Place the pan directly in the pot. Close the hood and AIR CRISP for 7 minutes.
3. In a separate bowl, mix the sour cream, mayonnaise, salt, pepper, and basil using a whisk.
4. Coat the salad with the dressing and serve.

Crispy Pork Tenderloin

Servings: 6
Cooking Time: 10 Minutes
Ingredients:

- 2 large egg whites
- 1½ tablespoons Dijon mustard
- 2 cups crushed pretzel crumbs
- 1½ pounds pork tenderloin, cut into ¼-pound sections
- Cooking spray

Directions:
1. Spritz the Crisper Basket with cooking spray.
2. Insert the Crisper Basket and close the hood. Select AIR CRISP, set the temperature to 350°F, and set the time to 10 minutes. Select START/STOP to begin preheating.
3. Whisk the egg whites with Dijon mustard in a bowl until bubbly. Pour the pretzel crumbs in a separate bowl.
4. Dredge the pork tenderloin in the egg white mixture and press to coat. Shake the excess off and roll the tenderloin over the pretzel crumbs.
5. Arrange the well-coated pork tenderloin in batches in a single layer in the Crisper Basket and spritz with cooking spray.
6. Close the hood and AIR CRISP for 10 minutes or until the pork is golden brown and crispy. Flip the pork halfway through. Repeat with remaining pork sections.
7. Serve immediately.

Easy Beef Schnitzel

Servings: 1
Cooking Time: 12 Minutes
Ingredients:

- ½ cup friendly bread crumbs
- 2 tablespoons olive oil
- Pepper and salt, to taste
- 1 egg, beaten
- 1 thin beef schnitzel

Directions:
1. Insert the Crisper Basket and close the hood. Select AIR CRISP, set the temperature to 350°F, and set the time to 12 minutes. Select START/STOP to begin preheating.
2. In a shallow dish, combine the bread crumbs, oil, pepper, and salt.
3. In a second shallow dish, place the beaten egg.
4. Dredge the schnitzel in the egg before rolling it in the bread crumbs.
5. Put the coated schnitzel in the Crisper Basket. Close the hood and AIR CRISP for 12 minutes. Flip the schnitzel halfway through.
6. Serve immediately.

Apple-glazed Pork

Servings: 4
Cooking Time: 19 Minutes

Ingredients:

- 1 sliced apple
- 1 small onion, sliced
- 2 tablespoons apple cider vinegar, divided
- ½ teaspoon thyme
- ½ teaspoon rosemary
- ¼ teaspoon brown sugar
- 3 tablespoons olive oil, divided
- ¼ teaspoon smoked paprika
- 4 pork chops
- Salt and ground black pepper, to taste

Directions:

1. Select BAKE, set the temperature to 350°F, and set the time to 4 minutes. Select START/STOP to begin preheating.

2. Combine the apple slices, onion, 1 tablespoon of vinegar, thyme, rosemary, brown sugar, and 2 tablespoons of olive oil in a baking pan. Stir to mix well.

3. Place the pan directly in the pot. Close the hood and BAKE for 4 minutes.

4. Meanwhile, combine the remaining vinegar and olive oil, and paprika in a large bowl. Sprinkle with salt and ground black pepper. Stir to mix well. Dredge the pork in the mixture and toss to coat well.

5. Remove the baking pan from the grill and put in the pork. Place the pan directly in the pot. Close the hood and AIR CRISP for 10 minutes to lightly brown the pork. Flip the pork chops halfway through.

6. Remove the pork from the grill and baste with baked apple mixture on both sides. Put the pork back to the grill and AIR CRISP for an additional 5 minutes. Flip halfway through.

7. Serve immediately.

Pork Chops In Bourbon

Servings: 4
Cooking Time: 35 Minutes

Ingredients:

- 2 cups ketchup
- ¾ cup bourbon
- ¼ cup apple cider vinegar
- ¼ cup soy sauce
- 1 cup packed brown sugar
- 3 tablespoons Worcestershire sauce
- ½ tablespoon dry mustard powder
- 4 boneless pork chops
- Sea salt, to taste
- Freshly ground black pepper, to taste

Directions:

1. In a medium saucepan over high heat, combine the ketchup, bourbon, vinegar, soy sauce, sugar, Worcestershire sauce, and mustard powder. Stir to combine and bring to a boil.

2. Reduce the heat to low and simmer, uncovered and stirring occasionally, for 20 minutes. The barbecue sauce will thicken while cooking. Once thickened, remove the pan from the heat and set aside.

3. While the barbecue sauce is cooking, insert the Grill Grate into the unit and close the hood. Select GRILL, set the temperature to MEDIUM, and set the time to 15 minutes. Select START/STOP to begin preheating.

4. When the unit beeps to signify it has preheated, place the pork chops on the Grill Grate. Close the hood, and GRILL for 8 minutes. After 8 minutes, flip the pork chops and baste the cooked side with the barbecue sauce. Close the hood, and GRILL for 5 minutes more.

5. Open the hood, and flip the pork chops again, basting both sides with the barbecue sauce. Close the hood, and GRILL for the final 2 minutes.

6. When cooking is complete, season with salt and pepper and serve immediately.

Tomato And Lamb Stew

Servings: 6
Cooking Time: 1 Hour
Ingredients:

- 2 tablespoons unsalted butter
- 1 yellow onion, diced
- 4 garlic cloves, minced
- 2 pounds lamb shoulder roast, cut into 1-inch cubes
- 3 cups beef broth
- 1 large potato, cubed
- 1 medium carrot, sliced
- 3 bay leaves
- Salt
- Freshly ground black pepper
- 1 (8-ounce) can tomato sauce
- 1 red bell pepper, chopped
- 1 green bell pepper, chopped

Directions:

1. Insert the Cooking Pot and close the hood. Select ROAST, set the temperature to 350°F, and set the time to 1 hour. Select START/STOP to begin preheating.

2. When the unit beeps to signify it has preheated, place the butter, onion, and garlic in the Cooking Pot. Then add the lamb and stir with a wooden spoon. Close the hood and cook for 10 minutes.

3. After 10 minutes, open the hood and add the beef broth, potato, carrot, and bay leaves, and then season with salt and pepper. Stir to combine. Close the hood and cook for 20 minutes.

4. After 20 minutes, open the hood and stir in the tomato sauce. Close the hood and cook for 10 minutes. After 10 minutes, open the hood and stir. Close the hood and cook for 10 minutes. After 10 minutes, open the hood and add the bell peppers. Close the hood and cook for 10 minutes more.

5. When cooking is complete, open the hood, stir the stew, and remove the bay leaves. Transfer to bowls and serve.

Spicy Beef Lettuce Wraps

Servings: 4
Cooking Time: 10 Minutes
Ingredients:

- 1 pound ground beef
- 1 tablespoon sesame oil
- 1 tablespoon minced garlic
- 1 teaspoon peeled minced fresh ginger
- 3 tablespoons light brown sugar, packed
- ¼ cup soy sauce
- 1 teaspoon salt
- ½ teaspoon freshly ground black pepper
- 2 teaspoons sriracha
- 1 red chile, thinly sliced, or ¼ teaspoon red pepper flakes
- ½ cup sliced scallions, both white and green parts
- 12 butter lettuce leaves

Directions:

1. Insert the Cooking Pot and close the hood. Select GRILL, set the temperature to HI, and set the time to 10 minutes. Select START/STOP to begin preheating.

2. When the unit beeps to signify it has preheated, place the ground beef in the Cooking Pot. Carefully break the ground beef apart with a wooden spoon or spatula. Stir in the sesame oil, garlic, and ginger. Close the hood and cook for 5 minutes.

3. After 5 minutes, open the hood and stir the ground beef. Stir in the brown sugar, soy sauce, salt, pepper, and sriracha. Close the hood and cook for 5 minutes more.

4. When cooking is complete, open the hood and stir in the chile and scallions. Close the hood and let sit for about 3 minutes for the mixture to set.

5. Scoop the ground beef mixture into the lettuce leaves and serve.

Vietnamese Pork Chops

Servings: 2
Cooking Time: 12 Minutes
Ingredients:

- 1 tablespoon chopped shallot
- 1 tablespoon chopped garlic
- 1 tablespoon fish sauce
- 3 tablespoons lemongrass
- 1 teaspoon soy sauce
- 1 tablespoon brown sugar
- 1 tablespoon olive oil
- 1 teaspoon ground black pepper
- 2 pork chops

Directions:

1. Combine shallot, garlic, fish sauce, lemongrass, soy sauce, brown sugar, olive oil, and pepper in a bowl. Stir to mix well.
2. Put the pork chops in the bowl. Toss to coat well. Place the bowl in the refrigerator to marinate for 2 hours.
3. Insert the Crisper Basket and close the hood. Select AIR CRISP, set the temperature to 400°F, and set the time to 12 minutes. Select START/STOP to begin preheating.
4. Remove the pork chops from the bowl and discard the marinade. Transfer the chops into the basket.
5. Close the hood and AIR CRISP for 12 minutes or until lightly browned. Flip the pork chops halfway through the cooking time.
6. Remove the pork chops from the basket and serve hot.

Rosemary And Garlic Lamb Pitas

Servings: 6
Cooking Time: 12 Minutes
Ingredients:

- For the lamb
- ¼ cup extra-virgin olive oil
- 1 tablespoon garlic powder
- 2 garlic cloves, minced
- 2 teaspoons onion powder
- Juice of ½ lemon
- ¼ teaspoon nutmeg
- 2 tablespoons fresh rosemary
- 1 teaspoon salt
- 2 pounds boneless lamb, thinly sliced
- 6 pitas
- For the tzatziki sauce
- 2 cups Greek yogurt
- 1 tablespoon garlic powder
- ¼ teaspoon onion powder
- 2 teaspoons salt
- 2 tablespoons fresh dill
- 2 tablespoons freshly squeezed lemon juice
- ⅛ teaspoon freshly ground black pepper
- 1 tablespoon extra-virgin olive oil
- 1 cucumber, seeded and diced

Directions:

1. In a large bowl, whisk together the olive oil, garlic powder, minced garlic, onion powder, lemon juice, nutmeg, rosemary, and salt. Add the lamb and massage the mixture into the meat. Cover and marinate for 30 minutes.
2. Insert the Grill Grate and close the hood. Select GRILL, set the temperature to HI, and set the time to 12 minutes. Select START/STOP to begin preheating.
3. When the unit beeps to signify it has preheated, place the lamb slices on the Grill Grate in a single layer. Close the hood and cook for 6 minutes.
4. After 6 minutes, open the hood and flip the meat. Close the hood and cook for 6 minutes more.
5. While the lamb is cooking, in a medium bowl, combine the yogurt, garlic powder, onion powder, salt, dill, lemon juice, pepper, and olive oil. Add the cucumber and mix well.
6. Serve the lamb inside warm pita pockets and top with tzatziki sauce.

Mozzarella Meatball Sandwiches With Basil

Servings: 4

Cooking Time: 10 Minutes

Ingredients:

- 12 frozen meatballs
- 8 slices Mozzarella cheese
- 4 sub rolls, halved lengthwise
- ½ cup marinara sauce, warmed
- 12 fresh basil leaves

Directions:

1. Insert the Crisper Basket and close the hood. Select AIR CRISP, set the temperature to 350°F, and set the time to 10 minutes. Select START/STOP to begin preheating.

2. When the unit beeps to signify it has preheated, place the meatballs in the basket. Close the hood and AIR CRISP for 5 minutes.

3. After 5 minutes, shake the basket of meatballs. Place the basket back in the unit and close the hood to resume cooking.

4. While the meatballs are cooking, place two slices of Mozzarella cheese on each sub roll. Use a spoon to spread the marinara sauce on top of the cheese slices. Press three leaves of basil into the sauce on each roll.

5. When cooking is complete, place three meatballs on each sub roll. Serve immediately.

Pulled Pork Sandwiches

Servings: 6 To 8

Cooking Time: 1 Hour 30 Minutes

Ingredients:

- 1 tablespoon onion powder
- 1 tablespoon garlic powder
- 1 tablespoon salt
- 1 teaspoon freshly ground black pepper
- 1 teaspoon ground cumin
- 1 teaspoon ground cayenne pepper
- 3 tablespoons light brown sugar, packed
- 1 tablespoon granulated sugar
- 3 to 4 pounds pork shoulder, cut into 3 or 4 equal pieces
- 3 tablespoons unsalted butter, sliced
- 3 tablespoons honey
- 4 tablespoons barbecue sauce
- Hamburger buns or sandwich bread

Directions:

1. Plug the thermometer into the unit. Insert the Grill Grate and close the hood. Select ROAST, set the temperature to 350°F, and set the time to 90 minutes. Select START/STOP to begin preheating.

2. While the unit is preheating, in a small bowl, combine the onion powder, garlic powder, salt, black pepper, cumin, cayenne pepper, brown sugar, and granulated sugar. Rub the mixture on all sides of the pork pieces. Insert the Smart Thermometer into the thickest part of the meat.

3. When the unit beeps to signify it has preheated, place the pork on the Grill Grate. Manually select the temperature setting to reach 165°F. Close the hood and cook for 45 minutes or until the Smart Thermometer indicates the temperature has been reached.

4. When cooking is complete, open the hood and remove the Smart Thermometer. Use grill mitts to remove the Grill Grate and pork shoulder. Place the pork pieces on top of a large piece of aluminum foil. Top with the butter slices and drizzle with the honey and barbecue sauce. Close the foil over the pork and crimp it to seal.

5. Place the foil-wrapped pork in the Cooking Pot. Carefully pierce the foil to reinsert the Smart Thermometer in the thickest part of the meat. Manually select the temperature setting to reach 200°F. Close the hood and cook for 45 minutes.

6. When cooking is complete, the Smart Thermometer will indicate that the desired temperature has been reached. Open the hood and use grill mitts to remove the foil-wrapped pork. Let the meat rest in the foil for 30 minutes. Once it has rested, shred the pork using two forks and place some meat on top of a bun, topped with more barbecue sauce, if desired. Serve.

Bacon Burger Meatballs

Servings: 4
Cooking Time: 20 Minutes
Ingredients:

- 1 white onion, diced
- 1 pound thick-cut bacon (12 to 16 slices), cooked and crumbled
- 8 ounces cream cheese, at room temperature
- 4 tablespoons minced garlic
- ¼ cup ketchup
- ¼ cup yellow mustard
- ¼ cup gluten-free Worcestershire sauce
- 3 eggs
- 2 pounds ground beef

Directions:

1. In a large bowl, mix together the onion, bacon crumbles, cream cheese, garlic, ketchup, mustard, Worcestershire sauce, and eggs. Add the ground beef and, using your hands, mix the ingredients together until just combined, being careful to not overmix. Form the mixture into 1½- to 2-inch meatballs. This should make 20 to 22 meatballs.

2. Insert the Grill Grate and close the hood. Select GRILL, set the temperature to MED, and set the time to 20 minutes. Select START/STOP to begin preheating.

3. When the unit beeps to signify it has preheated, place the meatballs on the Grill Grate. Close the hood and cook for 10 minutes.

4. After 10 minutes, open the hood and flip the meatballs. Close the hood and cook for 10 minutes more.

5. When cooking is complete, remove the meatballs from the grill and serve.

Bacon-wrapped Sausage With Tomato Relish

Servings: 4
Cooking Time: 32 Minutes
Ingredients:

- 8 pork sausages
- 8 bacon strips
- Relish:
- 8 large tomatoes, chopped
- 1 small onion, peeled
- 1 clove garlic, peeled
- 1 tablespoon white wine vinegar
- 3 tablespoons chopped parsley
- 1 teaspoon smoked paprika
- 2 tablespoons sugar
- Salt and ground black pepper, to taste

Directions:

1. Purée the tomatoes, onion, and garlic in a food processor until well mixed and smooth.

2. Pour the purée in a saucepan and drizzle with white wine vinegar. Sprinkle with salt and ground black pepper. Simmer over medium heat for 10 minutes.

3. Add the parsley, paprika, and sugar to the saucepan and cook for 10 more minutes or until it has a thick consistency. Keep stirring during the cooking. Refrigerate for an hour to chill.

4. Insert the Crisper Basket and close the hood. Select AIR CRISP, set the temperature to 350°F, and set the time to 12 minutes. Select START/STOP to begin preheating.

5. Wrap the sausage with bacon strips and secure with toothpicks, then place them in the basket.

6. Close the hood and AIR CRISP for 12 minutes or until the bacon is crispy and browned. Flip the bacon-wrapped sausage halfway through.

7. Transfer the bacon-wrapped sausage on a plate and baste with the relish or just serve with the relish alongside.

Korean-style Steak Tips

Servings: 4
Cooking Time: 13 Minutes
Ingredients:

- 4 garlic cloves, minced
- ½ apple, peeled and grated
- 3 tablespoons sesame oil
- 3 tablespoons brown sugar

- ⅓ cup soy sauce
- 1 teaspoon freshly ground black pepper
- Sea salt
- 1½ pounds beef tips

Directions:

1. In a medium bowl, combine the garlic, apple, sesame oil, sugar, soy sauce, pepper, and salt until well mixed.
2. Place the beef tips in a large shallow bowl and pour the marinade over them. Cover and refrigerate for 30 minutes.
3. Insert the Grill Grate and close the hood. Select GRILL, set the temperature to MEDIUM, and set the time to 13 minutes. Select START/STOP to begin preheating.
4. When the unit beeps to signify it has preheated, place the steak tips on the Grill Grate. Close the hood and GRILL for 11 minutes.
5. Cooking is complete to medium doneness when the internal temperature of the meat reaches 145ºF on a food thermometer. If desired, GRILL for up to 2 minutes more.
6. Remove the steak, and set it on a cutting board to rest for 5 minutes. Serve.

Lamb Rack With Pistachio

Servings: 2
Cooking Time: 20 Minutes
Ingredients:

- ½ cup finely chopped pistachios
- 1 teaspoon chopped fresh rosemary
- 3 tablespoons panko breadcrumbs
- 2 teaspoons chopped fresh oregano

- 1 tablespoon olive oil
- Salt and freshly ground black pepper, to taste
- 1 lamb rack, bones fat trimmed and frenched
- 1 tablespoon Dijon mustard

Directions:

1. Insert the Crisper Basket and close the hood. Select AIR CRISP, set the temperature to 380ºF, and set the time to 12 minutes. Select START/STOP to begin preheating.
2. Put the pistachios, rosemary, breadcrumbs, oregano, olive oil, salt, and black pepper in a food processor. Pulse to combine until smooth.
3. Rub the lamb rack with salt and black pepper on a clean work surface, then place it in the basket.
4. Close the hood and AIR CRISP for 12 minutes or until lightly browned. Flip the lamb halfway through the cooking time.
5. Transfer the lamb to a plate and brush with Dijon mustard on the fat side, then sprinkle with the pistachios mixture over the lamb rack to coat well.
6. Put the lamb rack back to the basket. Close the hood and AIR CRISP for 8 more minutes or until the internal temperature of the rack reaches at least 145ºF.
7. Remove the lamb rack from the grill with tongs and allow to cool for 5 minutes before sling to serve.

Sweet And Tangy Beef

Servings: 4
Cooking Time: 12 Minutes
Ingredients:

- For the beef
- 2 pounds top sirloin steak, thinly sliced
- 1 tablespoon cornstarch
- 3 tablespoons avocado oil
- 3 tablespoons soy sauce
- 2 tablespoons oyster sauce
- 1 tablespoon peeled minced fresh ginger
- 1 tablespoon sesame oil
- ½ teaspoon salt
- 1 onion, coarsely chopped
- 1 red bell pepper, coarsely chopped
- For the sweet and tangy sauce
- ½ cup water
- 2 tablespoons ketchup
- 2 tablespoons oyster sauce
- 2 tablespoons light brown sugar, packed
- 1 teaspoon salt
- 1 teaspoon sesame oil
- 1 tablespoon white vinegar
- 1 tablespoon Worcestershire sauce

Directions:

1. Insert the Cooking Pot and close the hood. Select GRILL, set the temperature to HI, and set the time to 12 minutes. Select START/STOP to begin preheating.

2. In a large bowl, combine the beef, cornstarch, avocado oil, soy sauce, oyster sauce, ginger, sesame oil, and salt. Mix well so the beef slices are fully coated.

3. When the unit beeps to signify it has preheated, transfer the beef to the Cooking Pot. Close the hood and cook for 6 minutes.

4. While the beef is cooking, in a small bowl, combine the water, ketchup, oyster sauce, brown sugar, salt, sesame oil, vinegar, and Worcestershire sauce. Stir until the sugar is dissolved.

5. After 6 minutes, open the hood and stir the beef. Add the onion and red bell pepper to the Cooking Pot. Close the hood and cook for 2 minutes. After 2 minutes, open the hood and add the sauce to the pot. Close the hood and cook for 4 minutes more.

6. When cooking is complete, spoon the beef and sauce over white rice, if desired. Serve.

Green Curry Beef

Servings: 4
Cooking Time: 12 Minutes
Ingredients:

- 1 yellow onion
- 1 red bell pepper
- 2 pounds sirloin steak
- 1 tablespoon minced garlic
- 1 tablespoon light brown sugar, packed
- 2 tablespoons green curry paste
- 1 teaspoon salt
- ½ teaspoon freshly ground black pepper
- Juice of ½ lime
- 1 (13-ounce) can full-fat unsweetened coconut milk
- 2 tablespoons fish sauce (optional)
- 1 cup fresh Thai basil or sweet basil

Directions:

1. Insert the Cooking Pot and close the hood. Select GRILL, set the temperature to MED, and set the time to 12 minutes. Select START/STOP to begin preheating.

2. While the unit is preheating, dice the onion, slice the red bell pepper, and thinly slice the steak into bite-size strips.

3. When the unit beeps to signify it has preheated, place the onion and garlic in the Cooking Pot. Then add the beef and stir with a wooden spoon. Close the hood and cook for 4 minutes.

4. After 4 minutes, open the hood and add the brown sugar, green curry paste, salt, pepper, lime juice, coconut milk, and fish sauce (if using). Close the hood and cook for 4 minutes. After 4 minutes, open the hood and stir the curry. Close the hood and cook for 4 minutes more.

5. When cooking is complete, open the hood, add the basil, and stir one more time. Close the hood and let the coconut curry sit for 5 minutes before serving.

Teriyaki Pork And Mushroom Rolls

Servings: 6
Cooking Time: 8 Minutes

Ingredients:

- 4 tablespoons brown sugar
- 4 tablespoons mirin
- 4 tablespoons soy sauce
- 1 teaspoon almond flour
- 2-inch ginger, chopped
- 6 pork belly slices
- 6 ounces Enoki mushrooms

Directions:

1. Mix the brown sugar, mirin, soy sauce, almond flour, and ginger together until brown sugar dissolves.
2. Take pork belly slices and wrap around a bundle of mushrooms. Brush each roll with teriyaki sauce. Chill for half an hour.
3. Insert the Crisper Basket and close the hood. Select AIR CRISP, set the temperature to 350°F, and set the time to 8 minutes. Select START/STOP to begin preheating.
4. Add marinated pork rolls to the basket.
5. Close the hood and AIR CRISP for 8 minutes. Flip the rolls halfway through.
6. Serve immediately.

Sizzling Pork Sisig

Servings: 6 To 8
Cooking Time: 50 Minutes

Ingredients:

- 3 pounds pork shoulder or pork belly, cut into 1-inch-thick slices
- 2 tablespoons soy sauce
- 2 tablespoons rice vinegar
- 2 tablespoons fish sauce
- Juice of 1 lemon, divided
- 1 tablespoon garlic powder
- ¼ teaspoon peeled minced fresh ginger
- 1 small red onion, diced
- 2 red Thai chiles, sliced

Directions:

1. Insert the Cooking Pot and close the hood. Select ROAST, set the temperature to 350°F, and set the time to 30 minutes. Select START/STOP to begin preheating.
2. When the unit beeps to signify it has preheated, place the pork in the Cooking Pot. Close the hood and cook for 15 minutes.
3. After 15 minutes, open the hood and flip the pork. Close the hood and cook for 15 minutes more.
4. When cooking is complete, remove the pork and set aside to cool.
5. While the pork is cooling, prepare the sauce. In a small bowl, combine the soy sauce, vinegar, fish sauce, juice of ½ lemon, garlic powder, and ginger. Place the diced onion and sliced chiles in a separate small bowl and set aside. Once the pork has cooled down enough to handle, cut the pork into ½-inch cubes.
6. Wash and dry the Cooking Pot. Then insert the Cooking Pot and close the hood. Select GRILL, set the temperature to HI, and set the time to 20 minutes. Select START/STOP to begin preheating.
7. When the unit beeps to signify it has preheated, place the pork in the Cooking Pot. Close the hood and cook for 10 minutes.
8. After 10 minutes, open the hood, stir the pork, and pour in the sauce. Close the hood and cook for 10 minutes more.
9. When cooking is complete, transfer the pork and sauce to a bowl. Add the onion and chiles on top and squeeze the juice of the remaining ½ lemon over the top. Serve.

Balsamic Honey Mustard Lamb Chops

Servings: 4 To 6
Cooking Time: 45 Minutes To 1 Hour
Ingredients:

- ¼ cup avocado oil
- ½ cup balsamic vinegar
- 2 garlic cloves, minced
- 1 teaspoon salt
- ½ teaspoon freshly ground black pepper
- 2 tablespoons honey
- 1 tablespoon yellow mustard
- 1 tablespoon fresh rosemary
- 1 (2- to 3-pound) rack of lamb

Directions:

1. In a large bowl, whisk together the avocado oil, vinegar, garlic, salt, pepper, honey, mustard, and rosemary. Add the lamb and massage and coat all sides of the meat with the marinade. Cover and refrigerate for at least 1 hour.
2. Plug the thermometer into the unit. Insert the Cooking Pot and close the hood. Select ROAST, set the temperature to 350°F, and select PRESET. Use the arrows to the right to select BEEF/ LAMB. The unit will default to WELL to cook lamb to a safe temperature. Insert the Smart Thermometer in the thickest part of the lamb without touching bone. Select START/STOP to begin preheating.
3. When the unit beeps to signify it has preheated, place the rack of lamb in the Cooking Pot. Close the hood to begin cooking.
4. When cooking is complete, the Smart Thermometer will indicate that the specified internal temperature has been reached. Remove the lamb from the pot and serve.

Crackling Pork Roast

Servings: 8
Cooking Time: 1 Hour 30 Minutes
Ingredients:

- 1 (3- to 4-pound) boneless pork shoulder, rind on
- Kosher salt

Directions:

1. Pat the roast dry with a paper towel. Using a sharp knife, score the rind, creating a diamond pattern on top. Season generously with salt. Place it in the refrigerator, uncovered, overnight to brine.
2. Plug the thermometer into the unit. Insert the Cooking Pot and close the hood. Select ROAST, set the temperature to 350°F, then select PRESET. Use the arrows to the right to select PORK. The unit will default to WELL to cook pork to a safe temperature. Insert the Smart Thermometer into the thickest part of the meat. Select START/STOP to begin preheating.
3. When the unit beeps to signify it has preheated, place the roast in the Cooking Pot. Close the hood to begin cooking.
4. When cooking is complete, the Smart Thermometer will indicate that the desired temperature has been reached. Remove the pork and let it rest for 10 minutes before slicing.

Rack Of Lamb Chops With Rosemary

Servings: 2
Cooking Time: 14 Minutes
Ingredients:

- 3 tablespoons extra-virgin olive oil
- 1 garlic clove, minced
- 1 tablespoon fresh rosemary, chopped
- ½ rack lamb
- Sea salt, to taste
- Freshly ground black pepper, to taste

Directions:

1. Combine the oil, garlic, and rosemary in a large bowl. Season the rack of lamb with the salt and pepper, then place the lamb in the bowl, using tongs to turn and coat fully in the oil mixture. Cover and refrigerate for 2 hours.
2. Insert the Grill Grate and close the hood. Select GRILL, set the temperature to HIGH, and set the time to 14 minutes. Select START/STOP to begin preheating.
3. When the unit beeps to signify it has preheated, place the lamb on the Grill Grate. Close the hood and GRILL for 6 minutes. After 6 minutes, flip the lamb and continue grilling for 6 minutes more.
4. Cooking is complete when the internal temperature of the lamb reaches 145°F on a food thermometer. If needed, GRILL for up to 2 minutes more.

Fast Lamb Satay

Servings: 2
Cooking Time: 8 Minutes
Ingredients:

- ¼ teaspoon cumin
- 1 teaspoon ginger
- ½ teaspoons nutmeg
- Salt and ground black pepper, to taste
- 2 boneless lamb steaks
- Cooking spray

Directions:

1. Combine the cumin, ginger, nutmeg, salt and pepper in a bowl.
2. Cube the lamb steaks and massage the spice mixture into each one.
3. Leave to marinate for 10 minutes, then transfer onto metal skewers.
4. Insert the Crisper Basket and close the hood. Select AIR CRISP, set the temperature to 400°F, and set the time to 8 minutes. Select START/STOP to begin preheating.
5. Place the skewers in the basket and spritz with cooking spray. Close the hood and AIR CRISP for 8 minutes.
6. Take care when removing them from the grill and serve.

Beef And Vegetable Cubes

Servings: 4
Cooking Time: 17 Minutes
Ingredients:

- 2 tablespoons olive oil
- 1 tablespoon apple cider vinegar
- 1 teaspoon fine sea salt
- ½ teaspoons ground black pepper
- 1 teaspoon shallot powder
- ¾ teaspoon smoked cayenne pepper
- ½ teaspoons garlic powder
- ¼ teaspoon ground cumin
- 1 pound top round steak, cut into cubes
- 4 ounces broccoli, cut into florets
- 4 ounces mushrooms, sliced
- 1 teaspoon dried basil
- 1 teaspoon celery seeds

Directions:

1. Massage the olive oil, vinegar, salt, black pepper, shallot powder, cayenne pepper, garlic powder, and cumin into the cubed steak, ensuring to coat each piece evenly.
2. Allow to marinate for a minimum of 3 hours.
3. Insert the Crisper Basket and close the hood. Select AIR CRISP, set the temperature to 365°F, and set the time to 12 minutes. Select START/STOP to begin preheating.
4. Put the beef cubes in the Crisper Basket. Close the hood and AIR CRISP for 12 minutes.
5. When the steak is cooked through, place it in a bowl.
6. Wipe the grease from the basket and pour in the vegetables. Season them with basil and celery seeds.
7. Increase the temperature of the grill to 400°F and AIR CRISP for 5 to 6 minutes. When the vegetables are hot, serve them with the steak.

Baby Back Ribs In Gochujang Marinade

Servings: 4
Cooking Time: 22 Minutes
Ingredients:

- ¼ cup gochujang paste
- ¼ cup soy sauce
- ¼ cup freshly squeezed orange juice
- 2 tablespoons apple cider vinegar
- 2 tablespoons sesame oil
- 6 garlic cloves, minced
- 1½ tablespoons brown sugar
- 1 tablespoon grated fresh ginger
- 1 teaspoon salt
- 4 baby back ribs

Directions:

1. In a medium bowl, add the gochujang paste, soy sauce, orange juice, vinegar, oil, garlic, sugar, ginger, and salt, and stir to combine.
2. Place the baby back ribs on a baking sheet and coat all sides with the sauce. Cover with aluminum foil and refrigerate for 6 hours.
3. Insert the Grill Grate and close the hood. Select GRILL, set the temperature to MEDIUM, and set the time to 22 minutes. Select START/STOP to begin preheating.
4. When the unit beeps to signify it has preheated, place the ribs on the Grill Grate. Close the hood and GRILL for 11 minutes. After 11 minutes, flip the ribs, close the hood, and GRILL for an additional 11 minutes.
5. When cooking is complete, serve immediately.

Spaghetti Squash Lasagna

Servings: 6
Cooking Time: 1 Hour 15 Minutes
Ingredients:

- 2 large spaghetti squash, cooked
- 4 pounds ground beef
- 1 large jar Marinara sauce
- 25 slices Mozzarella cheese
- 30 ounces whole-milk ricotta cheese

Directions:

1. Select BAKE, set the temperature to 375°F, and set the time to 45 minutes. Select START/STOP to begin preheating.
2. Slice the spaghetti squash and place it face down inside a baking pan. Fill with water until covered.
3. Place the pan directly in the pot. Close the hood and BAKE for 45 minutes until skin is soft.
4. Sear the ground beef in a skillet over medium-high heat for 5 minutes or until browned, then add the marinara sauce and heat until warm. Set aside.
5. Scrape the flesh off the cooked squash to resemble strands of spaghetti.
6. Layer the lasagna in a large greased pan in alternating layers of spaghetti squash, beef sauce, Mozzarella, ricotta. Repeat until all the ingredients have been used.
7. Place the pan directly in the pot. Close the hood and BAKE for 30 minutes.
8. Serve.

Uncle's Famous Tri-tip

Servings: 6 To 8
Cooking Time: 20 Minutes
Ingredients:

- ¼ cup avocado oil
- ½ cup red wine vinegar
- ¼ cup light brown sugar, packed
- 4 tablespoons honey mustard
- 1 tablespoon garlic powder
- 1 tablespoon onion powder
- 1 tablespoon paprika
- 1 tablespoon salt
- 1 tablespoon freshly ground black pepper
- 3 pounds tri-tip

Directions:

1. In a large resealable bag, combine the avocado oil, red wine vinegar, brown sugar, honey mustard, garlic powder, onion powder, paprika, salt, and pepper. Add the tri-tip, seal, and massage the mixture into the meat. Refrigerate overnight.
2. About 20 minutes before grilling, remove the bag from the refrigerator so the marinade becomes liquid again at room temperature.
3. Plug the thermometer into the unit. Insert the Grill Grate and close the hood. Select GRILL, set the temperature to MED, and select PRESET. Use the arrows to the right to select BEEF, then choose desired doneness. Insert the Smart Thermometer into the thickest part of the meat. Select START/STOP to begin preheating.
4. When the unit beeps to signify it has preheated, place the tri-tip on the Grill Grate, fat-side up. Close the hood to begin cooking.
5. When the Foodi™ Grill indicates it is time to flip, open the hood and flip the tri-tip. Close the hood and continue cooking until the Smart Thermometer indicates your desired internal temperature has been reached.
6. When cooking is complete, remove the tri-tip from the grill. Let rest for 10 minutes before slicing against the grain. Serve.

Swedish Beef Meatballs

Servings: 8
Cooking Time: 12 Minutes
Ingredients:

- 1 pound ground beef
- 1 egg, beaten
- 2 carrots, shredded
- 2 bread slices, crumbled
- 1 small onion, minced
- ½ teaspoons garlic salt
- Pepper and salt, to taste
- 1 cup tomato sauce
- 2 cups pasta sauce

Directions:

1. Insert the Crisper Basket and close the hood. Select AIR CRISP, set the temperature to 400°F, and set the time to 7 minutes. Select START/STOP to begin preheating.
2. In a bowl, combine the ground beef, egg, carrots, crumbled bread, onion, garlic salt, pepper and salt.
3. Divide the mixture into equal amounts and shape each one into a small meatball.
4. Put them in the Crisper Basket. Close the hood and AIR CRISP for 7 minutes.
5. Transfer the meatballs to an oven-safe dish and top with the tomato sauce and pasta sauce.
6. Set the dish into the pot and allow to AIR CRISP at 320°F for 5 more minutes. Serve hot.

Steak And Lettuce Salad

Servings: 4 To 6
Cooking Time: 16 Minutes
Ingredients:

- 4 skirt steaks
- Sea salt, to taste
- Freshly ground black pepper, to taste
- 6 cups chopped romaine lettuce
- ¾ cup cherry tomatoes, halved
- ¼ cup blue cheese, crumbled
- 1 cup croutons
- 2 avocados, peeled and sliced
- 1 cup blue cheese dressing

Directions:

1. Insert the Grill Grate and close the hood. Select GRILL, set the temperature to HIGH, and set the time to 8 minutes. Select START/STOP to begin preheating.

2. Season the steaks on both sides with the salt and pepper.

3. When the unit beeps to signify it has preheated, place 2 steaks on the Grill Grate. Gently press the steaks down to maximize grill marks. Close the hood and GRILL for 4 minutes. After 4 minutes, flip the steaks, close the hood, and GRILL for an additional 4 minutes.

4. Remove the steaks from the grill and transfer to them a cutting board. Tent with aluminum foil.

5. Repeat step 3 with the remaining 2 steaks.

6. While the second set of steaks is cooking, assemble the salad by tossing together the lettuce, tomatoes, blue cheese crumbles, and croutons. Top with the avocado slices.

7. Once the second set of steaks has finished cooking, slice all four of the steaks into thin strips, and place on top of the salad. Drizzle with the blue cheese dressing and serve.

Pork Chops With Creamy Mushroom Sauce

Servings: 6
Cooking Time: 10 Minutes
Ingredients:

- 1 cup heavy (whipping) cream
- ½ cup chicken broth
- 1 tablespoon cornstarch
- 1 teaspoon garlic powder
- 6 (6-ounce) boneless pork chops
- 8 ounces mushrooms, sliced

Directions:

1. Insert the Grill Grate and close the hood. Select GRILL, set the temperature to HI, and set the time to 10 minutes. Select START/STOP to begin preheating.

2. While the unit is preheating, in a medium bowl, whisk together the heavy cream, chicken broth, cornstarch, and garlic powder.

3. When the unit beeps to signify it has preheated, place the pork chops on the Grill Grate. Close the hood and grill for 5 minutes.

4. After 5 minutes, open the hood and use grill mitts to remove the Grill Grate and the chops. Pour the cream mixture into the Cooking Pot. Put the Grill Grate back into the unit and flip the pork chops. Close the hood and cook for 5 minutes more.

5. When cooking is complete, remove the pork chops from the grill. Use grill mitts to remove the Grill Grate from the unit and stir the cream mixture. Add the sliced mushrooms, close the hood, and let sit for 5 minutes. Pour the creamy mushroom sauce over the pork chops and serve.

Carne Asada Tacos

Servings: 4
Cooking Time: 15 Minutes
Ingredients:

- For the tacos
- ¼ cup avocado oil
- ¼ cup soy sauce
- ¼ cup orange juice
- 3 tablespoons white wine vinegar
- 3 tablespoons minced garlic
- Juice of 2 limes
- 1 teaspoon ground cumin
- 1 teaspoon salt
- 1 teaspoon freshly ground black pepper
- 1 teaspoon onion powder
- ½ cup chopped fresh cilantro
- 2 pounds skirt steak at least 1 inch thick
- 10 corn tortillas
- For the creamy cilantro sauce
- ¼ cup mayonnaise
- ¼ cup sour cream
- ¼ cup minced fresh cilantro, including stems
- Juice of 1 lime wedge, or more as desired
- ¼ teaspoon paprika
- ¼ teaspoon onion powder

Directions:

1. In a large bowl, whisk together the avocado oil, soy sauce, orange juice, vinegar, garlic, lime juice, cumin, salt, pepper, onion powder, and cilantro. Add the steak, making sure it is fully coated with the marinade. Set aside to marinate for 15 minutes.

2. Plug the thermometer into the unit. Insert the Grill Grate and close the hood. Select GRILL, set the temperature to HI, then select PRESET. Use the arrows to the right to select BEEF, then choose desired doneness. Insert the Smart Thermometer into the thickest part of the steak. Select START/STOP to begin preheating.

3. When the unit beeps to signify it has preheated, place the steak on the Grill Grate. Close the hood to begin cooking. The Foodi™ Grill will tell you when to flip the steak and when the desired internal temperature has been reached (15 minutes is for well-done steak).

4. While the steak is cooking, in a small bowl, combine the mayonnaise, sour cream, cilantro, lime juice, paprika, and onion powder.

5. When cooking is complete, remove the steak from the grill. Let it rest for 10 minutes before slicing against the grain. Serve in the tortillas and dress with the creamy cilantro sauce.

Smoky Paprika Pork And Vegetable Kabobs

Servings: 4
Cooking Time: 15 Minutes
Ingredients:

- 1 pound pork tenderloin, cubed
- 1 teaspoon smoked paprika
- Salt and ground black pepper, to taste
- 1 green bell pepper, cut into chunks
- 1 zucchini, cut into chunks
- 1 red onion, sliced
- 1 tablespoon oregano
- Cooking spray

Directions:

1. Spritz the Crisper Basket with cooking spray.

2. Insert the Crisper Basket and close the hood. Select AIR CRISP, set the temperature to 350ºF, and set the time to 15 minutes. Select START/STOP to begin preheating.

3. Add the pork to a bowl and season with the smoked paprika, salt and black pepper. Thread the seasoned pork cubes and vegetables alternately onto the soaked skewers.

4. Arrange the skewers in the prepared Crisper Basket and spray with cooking spray.

5. Close the hood and AIR CRISP for 15 minutes, or until the pork is well browned and the vegetables are tender, flipping once halfway through.

6. Transfer the skewers to the serving dishes and sprinkle with oregano. Serve hot.

Poultry Recipes

Pecan-crusted Turkey Cutlets

Servings: 4
Cooking Time: 10 To 12 Minutes
Ingredients:

- ¾ cup panko bread crumbs
- ¼ teaspoon salt
- ¼ teaspoon pepper
- ¼ teaspoon dry mustard
- ¼ teaspoon poultry seasoning
- ½ cup pecans
- ¼ cup cornstarch
- 1 egg, beaten
- 1 pound turkey cutlets, ½-inch thick
- Salt and pepper, to taste
- Cooking spray

Directions:

1. Insert the Crisper Basket and close the hood. Select AIR CRISP, set the temperature to 360°F, and set the time to 12 minutes. Select START/STOP to begin preheating.
2. Place the panko crumbs, salt, pepper, mustard, and poultry seasoning in a food processor. Process until crumbs are finely crushed. Add pecans and process just until nuts are finely chopped.
3. Place cornstarch in a shallow dish and beaten egg in another. Transfer coating mixture from food processor into a third shallow dish.
4. Sprinkle turkey cutlets with salt and pepper to taste.
5. Dip cutlets in cornstarch and shake off excess, then dip in beaten egg and finally roll in crumbs, pressing to coat well. Spray both sides with cooking spray.
6. Place 2 cutlets in Crisper Basket in a single layer. Close the hood and AIR CRISP for 10 to 12 minutes. Repeat with the remaining cutlets.
7. Serve warm.

Roasted Chicken Tenders With Veggies

Servings: 4
Cooking Time: 18 To 20 Minutes
Ingredients:

- 1 pound chicken tenders
- 1 tablespoon honey
- Pinch salt
- Freshly ground black pepper, to taste
- ½ cup soft fresh bread crumbs
- ½ teaspoon dried thyme
- 1 tablespoon olive oil
- 2 carrots, sliced
- 12 small red potatoes

Directions:

1. Insert the Crisper Basket and close the hood. Select ROAST, set the temperature to 380°F, and set the time to 20 minutes. Select START/STOP to begin preheating.
2. In a medium bowl, toss the chicken tenders with the honey, salt, and pepper.
3. In a shallow bowl, combine the bread crumbs, thyme, and olive oil, and mix.
4. Coat the tenders in the bread crumbs, pressing firmly onto the meat.
5. Place the carrots and potatoes in the Crisper Basket and top with the chicken tenders.
6. Close the hood and ROAST for 18 to 20 minutes, or until the chicken is cooked to 165°F and the vegetables are tender, shaking the basket halfway during the cooking time.
7. Serve warm.

Grilled Cornish Hens

Servings: 4
Cooking Time: 20 Minutes

Ingredients:

- ½ cup avocado oil
- 1 teaspoon dried oregano
- ½ teaspoon freshly ground black pepper
- 1 teaspoon garlic salt
- 2 tablespoons minced garlic
- 1 teaspoon chopped fresh thyme
- 1 teaspoon chopped fresh parsley
- 1 teaspoon chopped fresh rosemary
- 2 (1-pound) Cornish hens
- 1 large yellow onion, halved
- 4 garlic cloves, peeled

Directions:

1. Plug the thermometer into the unit. Insert the Grill Grate and close the hood. Select GRILL, set the temperature to LO, then select PRESET. Use the arrows to the right to select CHICKEN. The unit will default to WELL to cook poultry to a safe temperature. Select START/STOP to begin preheating.
2. While the unit is preheating, place the Smart Thermometer into the thickest part of the breast of one of the hens. In a small bowl, whisk together the avocado oil, oregano, pepper, garlic salt, minced garlic, thyme, parsley, and rosemary. Cut a few small slits in the skin of each Cornish hen. Rub the seasoning oil all over the skin and between the skin and meat where you made the slits. Place an onion half and 2 garlic cloves inside the cavity of each hen.
3. When the unit beeps to signify it has preheated, place the hens on the Grill Grate. Close the hood and cook.
4. When the Foodi™ Grill tells you, open the hood and flip the hens. Close the hood and continue to cook.
5. When cooking is complete, remove the hens from the grill and let sit for 5 minutes. Serve.

Lemony Chicken And Veggie Kebabs

Servings: 4
Cooking Time: 14 Minutes

Ingredients:

- 2 tablespoons plain Greek yogurt
- ¼ cup extra-virgin olive oil
- Juice of 4 lemons
- Grated zest of 1 lemon
- 4 garlic cloves, minced
- 2 tablespoons dried oregano
- 1 teaspoon sea salt
- ½ teaspoon freshly ground black pepper
- 1 pound boneless, skinless chicken breasts, cut into 2-inch cubes
- 1 red onion, quartered
- 1 zucchini, sliced

Directions:

1. In a large bowl, whisk together the Greek yogurt, oil, lemon juice, zest, garlic, oregano, salt, and pepper until well combined.
2. Place the chicken and half of the marinade into a large resealable plastic bag or container. Move the chicken around to coat evenly. Refrigerate for at least 30 minutes.
3. Insert the Grill Grate and close the hood. Select GRILL, set the temperature to MEDIUM, and set the time to 14 minutes. Select START/STOP to begin preheating.
4. While the unit is preheating, assemble the kebabs by threading the chicken on the wood skewers, alternating with the red onion and zucchini. Ensure the ingredients are pushed almost completely down to the end of the skewers.
5. When the unit beeps to signify it has preheated, place the skewers on the Grill Grate. Close hood and GRILL for 10 to 14 minutes, occasionally basting the kebabs with the remaining marinade while cooking.
6. Cooking is complete when the internal temperature of the chicken reaches 165°F on a food thermometer.

Sweet Chili Turkey Kebabs

Servings: 4
Cooking Time: 12 Minutes
Ingredients:

- 2 pounds turkey breast, cut into 1-inch cubes
- ¼ cup honey
- 1 tablespoon extra-virgin olive oil
- 2 tablespoons apple cider vinegar
- 2 tablespoons soy sauce
- Juice of 1 lime
- 1 teaspoon red pepper flakes

Directions:

1. Place 5 or 6 turkey cubes on each of 8 to 10 skewers. In a zip-top bag, combine the honey, olive oil, vinegar, soy sauce, lime juice, and red pepper flakes. Shake to mix well. Place the turkey skewers in the marinade and massage to coat the meat. Seal the bag and let marinate at room temperature for 30 minutes or in the refrigerator overnight.
2. Insert the Grill Grate and close the hood. Select GRILL, set the temperature to MED, and set the time to 12 minutes. Select START/STOP to begin preheating.
3. When the unit beeps to signify it has preheated, place half of the skewers on the Grill Grate. Brush extra glaze on the skewers. Close the hood and grill for 3 minutes.
4. After 3 minutes, open the hood and flip the skewers. Close the hood and cook for 3 minutes more.
5. After 3 minutes, remove the skewers from the grill. Repeat steps 3 and 4 for the remaining skewers.
6. When cooking is complete, remove the kebabs from the grill and serve.

Salsa Verde Chicken Enchiladas

Servings: 4
Cooking Time: 20 Minutes
Ingredients:

- 1 tablespoon chili powder
- 1 teaspoon onion powder
- 1 teaspoon garlic powder
- 1 teaspoon ground cumin
- 2 teaspoons salt
- 3 boneless, skinless chicken breasts (about 1½ pounds)
- Extra-virgin olive oil
- 1 (16-ounce) jar salsa verde
- 2 cups shredded Mexican-style cheese blend
- 6 (8-inch) flour tortillas
- Diced tomatoes, for topping
- Sour cream, for topping

Directions:

1. Insert the Grill Grate and close the hood. Select GRILL, set the temperature to MED, and set the time to 12 minutes. Select START/STOP to begin preheating.
2. While the unit is preheating, in a small bowl, combine the chili powder, onion powder, garlic powder, ground cumin, and salt. Drizzle the chicken breasts with the olive oil and season the meat on both sides with the seasoning mixture.
3. When the unit beeps to signify it has preheated, place the chicken breasts on the Grill Grate. Close the hood and cook for 6 minutes.
4. After 6 minutes, open the hood and flip the chicken. Close the hood and cook for 6 minutes more.
5. When cooking is complete, open the hood and use grill mitts to remove the Grill Grate and chicken breasts. Let the chicken breasts cool for about 5 minutes. Use two forks to shred the chicken, or cut it into small chunks.
6. To assemble the enchiladas, place a generous amount of chicken on a tortilla. Lift one end of the tortilla and roll it over and around the chicken. Do not fold in the sides of the tortilla as you roll. Place the enchilada, seam-side down, in the Cooking Pot. Repeat with the remaining 5 tortillas and the rest of the chicken. Pour the salsa verde over the enchiladas, completely covering them. Top the salsa with the shredded cheese.
7. Select BAKE, set the temperature to 350°F, and set the time to 8 minutes. Select START/STOP and then press the PREHEAT button to skip preheating. Close the hood and cook for 8 minutes.
8. When cooking is complete, remove the enchiladas from the pot and serve topped with the diced tomatoes and sour cream.

Stuffed Spinach Chicken Breast

Servings: 6
Cooking Time: 12 Minutes
Ingredients:

- 6 ounces cream cheese, at room temperature
- 1 teaspoon salt
- ½ teaspoon freshly ground black pepper
- ¼ cup mayonnaise
- 2 teaspoons garlic powder
- ½ cup grated Parmesan cheese
- 3 cups loosely packed spinach
- 1 teaspoon red pepper flakes (optional)
- 6 (6- to 8-ounce) boneless, skinless chicken breasts, butterflied (see here)
- Avocado oil

Directions:

1. Insert the Grill Grate and close the hood. Select GRILL, set the temperature to HI, and set the time to 12 minutes. Select START/STOP to begin preheating.

2. While the unit is preheating, in a large bowl, combine the cream cheese, salt, pepper, mayonnaise, garlic powder, Parmesan cheese, spinach, and red pepper flakes (if using). Spread the mixture inside the chicken breasts evenly. Close the breasts (like a book), enclosing the stuffing. Drizzle both sides of the chicken breasts with avocado oil for a nice coating.

3. When the unit beeps to signify it has preheated, place the chicken breasts on the Grill Grate. Close the hood and grill for 6 minutes.

4. After 6 minutes, open the hood and flip the chicken. Close the hood and cook for 6 minutes more.

5. When cooking is complete, open the hood and remove the chicken breasts from the grill. Serve.

Easy Asian Turkey Meatballs

Servings: 4
Cooking Time: 11 To 14 Minutes
Ingredients:

- 2 tablespoons peanut oil, divided
- 1 small onion, minced
- ¼ cup water chestnuts, finely chopped
- ½ teaspoon ground ginger
- 2 tablespoons low-sodium soy sauce
- ¼ cup panko bread crumbs
- 1 egg, beaten
- 1 pound ground turkey

Directions:

1. Select AIR CRISP, set the temperature to 400°F, and set the time to 2 minutes. Select START/STOP to begin preheating.

2. In a round metal pan, combine 1 tablespoon of peanut oil and onion. Place the pan directly in the pot. Close the hood and AIR CRISP for 1 to 2 minutes or until crisp and tender. Transfer the onion to a medium bowl.

3. Add the water chestnuts, ground ginger, soy sauce, and bread crumbs to the onion and mix well. Add egg and stir well. Mix in the ground turkey until combined.

4. Form the mixture into 1-inch meatballs. Drizzle the remaining 1 tablespoon of oil over the meatballs. Arrange the meatballs in the pan.

5. Place the pan directly in the pot. Close the hood and BAKE for 10 to 12 minutes, or until they are 165°F on a meat thermometer. Rest for 5 minutes before serving.

Teriyaki Chicken And Bell Pepper Kebabs

Servings: 4
Cooking Time: 14 Minutes
Ingredients:

- 1 pound boneless, skinless chicken breasts, cut into 2-inch cubes
- 1 cup teriyaki sauce, divided
- 2 green bell peppers, seeded and cut into 1-inch cubes
- 2 cups fresh pineapple, cut into 1-inch cubes

Directions:

1. Place the chicken and ½ cup of teriyaki sauce in a large resealable plastic bag or container. Toss to coat evenly. Refrigerate for at least 30 minutes.

2. Insert the Grill Grate and close the hood. Select GRILL, set the temperature to MEDIUM, and set the time to 14 minutes. Select START/STOP to begin preheating.

3. While the unit is preheating, assemble the kebabs by threading the chicken onto the wood skewers, alternating with the peppers and pineapple. Ensure the ingredients are pushed almost completely down to the end of the skewers.

4. When the unit beeps to signify it has preheated, place the skewers on the Grill Grate. Close the hood and GRILL for 10 to 14 minutes, occasionally basting the kebabs with the remaining ½ cup of teriyaki sauce while cooking.

5. Cooking is complete when the internal temperature of the chicken reaches 165°F on a food thermometer.

Buttermilk Ranch Chicken Tenders

Servings: 4
Cooking Time: 10 Minutes
Ingredients:

- 2 cups buttermilk
- 1 (0.4-ounce) packet ranch seasoning mix
- 1½ pounds boneless, skinless chicken breasts (about 3 breasts), cut into 1-inch strips
- 2 cups all-purpose flour
- ¼ teaspoon paprika
- ¼ teaspoon garlic powder
- ¼ teaspoon baking powder
- 2 teaspoons salt
- 2 large eggs
- ¼ cup avocado oil, divided

Directions:

1. In a large bowl, whisk together the buttermilk and ranch seasoning. Place the chicken strips in the bowl. Cover and let marinate in the refrigerator for 30 minutes.

2. Create an assembly line with 2 large bowls. Combine the flour, paprika, garlic powder, baking powder, and salt in one bowl. In the other bowl, whisk together the eggs. One at a time, remove the chicken strips from the marinade, shaking off any excess liquid. Dredge the chicken strip in the seasoned flour, coating both sides, then dip it in the beaten egg. Finally, dip it back into the seasoned flour bowl again. Shake any excess flour off. Repeat the process with all the chicken strips, setting them aside on a flat tray or plate once coated.

3. Insert the Grill Grate and close the hood. Select GRILL, set the temperature to MED, and set the time to 10 minutes. Select START/STOP to begin preheating.

4. While the unit is preheating, use a basting brush to generously coat one side of the chicken strips with half of the avocado oil.

5. When the unit beeps to signify it has preheated, place the chicken strips on the grill, oiled-side down. Brush the top of the chicken strips with the rest of the avocado oil. Close the hood and grill for 5 minutes.

6. After 5 minutes, open the hood and flip the chicken strips. Close the hood and continue cooking for 5 minutes more.

7. When cooking is complete, the chicken strips will be golden brown and crispy. Remove them from the grill and serve.

Dill Chicken Strips

Servings: 4

Cooking Time: 10 Minutes

Ingredients:

- 2 whole boneless, skinless chicken breasts, halved lengthwise
- 1 cup Italian dressing
- 3 cups finely crushed potato chips
- 1 tablespoon dried dill weed
- 1 tablespoon garlic powder
- 1 large egg, beaten
- Cooking spray

Directions:

1. In a large resealable bag, combine the chicken and Italian dressing. Seal the bag and refrigerate to marinate at least 1 hour.

2. In a shallow dish, stir together the potato chips, dill, and garlic powder. Place the beaten egg in a second shallow dish.

3. Remove the chicken from the marinade. Roll the chicken pieces in the egg and the potato chip mixture, coating thoroughly.

4. Select BAKE, set the temperature to 325°F, and set the time to 10 minutes. Select START/STOP to begin preheating.

5. Place the coated chicken in a baking pan and spritz with cooking spray.

6. Place the pan directly in the pot. Close the hood and BAKE for 5 minutes. Flip the chicken, spritz it with cooking spray, and bake for 5 minutes more until the outsides are crispy and the insides are no longer pink. Serve immediately.

Glazed Duck With Cherry Sauce

Servings: 12

Cooking Time: 32 Minutes

Ingredients:

- 1 whole duck, split in half, back and rib bones removed, fat trimmed
- 1 teaspoon olive oil
- Salt and freshly ground black pepper, to taste
- Cherry Sauce:
- 1 tablespoon butter
- 1 shallot, minced
- ½ cup sherry
- 1 cup chicken stock
- 1 teaspoon white wine vinegar
- ¾ cup cherry preserves
- 1 teaspoon fresh thyme leaves
- Salt and freshly ground black pepper, to taste

Directions:

1. Insert the Crisper Basket and close the hood. Select AIR CRISP, set the temperature to 400°F, and set the time to 25 minutes. Select START/STOP to begin preheating.

2. On a clean work surface, rub the duck with olive oil, then sprinkle with salt and ground black pepper to season.

3. Place the duck in the basket, breast side up. Close the hood and AIR CRISP for 25 minutes or until well browned. Flip the duck during the last 10 minutes.

4. Meanwhile, make the cherry sauce: Heat the butter in a nonstick skillet over medium-high heat or until melted.

5. Add the shallot and sauté for 5 minutes or until lightly browned.

6. Add the sherry and simmer for 6 minutes or until it reduces in half.

7. Add the chicken stick, white wine vinegar, and cherry preserves. Stir to combine well. Simmer for 6 more minutes or until thickened.

8. Fold in the thyme leaves and sprinkle with salt and ground black pepper. Stir to mix well.

9. When cooking of the duck is complete, glaze the duck with a quarter of the cherry sauce, then AIR CRISP for another 4 minutes.

10. Flip the duck and glaze with another quarter of the cherry sauce. AIR CRISP for an additional 3 minutes.

11. Transfer the duck on a large plate and serve with remaining cherry sauce.

Garlic Brown-butter Chicken With Tomatoes

Servings: 4

Cooking Time: 15 Minutes

Ingredients:

- 4 boneless, skinless chicken breasts
- Extra-virgin olive oil
- ½ teaspoon paprika
- ½ teaspoon sea salt
- 12 tablespoons (1½ sticks) unsalted butter
- 4 garlic cloves, minced
- 2 tablespoons light brown sugar, packed
- ½ teaspoon garlic powder
- 6 ounces cherry tomatoes

Directions:

1. Insert the Cooking Pot and close the hood. Select GRILL, set the temperature to MED, and set the time to 15 minutes. Select START/STOP to begin preheating.

2. While the unit is preheating, drizzle the chicken breasts with olive oil, then lightly sprinkle both sides with the paprika and salt.

3. When the unit beeps to signify it has preheated, place the butter and garlic in the Cooking Pot. Insert the Grill Grate on top and place the chicken breasts on the Grill Grate. Close the hood and grill for 8 minutes.

4. After 8 minutes, open the hood and use grill mitts to remove the Grill Grate and chicken. Add the brown sugar, garlic powder, and tomatoes to the butter and garlic and stir.

5. Transfer the chicken to the Cooking Pot, making sure you flip the breasts. Coat the chicken with the brown butter sauce. Close the hood and cook for 7 minutes more.

6. When cooking is complete, remove the chicken and place on a plate. Spoon the sauce over and serve.

Lime-garlic Grilled Chicken

Servings: 4

Cooking Time: 18 Minutes

Ingredients:

- 1½ tablespoons extra-virgin olive oil
- 3 garlic cloves, minced
- ¼ teaspoon ground cumin
- Sea salt, to taste
- Freshly ground black pepper, to taste
- Grated zest of 1 lime
- Juice of 1 lime
- 4 boneless, skinless chicken breasts

Directions:

1. In a large shallow bowl, stir together the oil, garlic, cumin, salt, pepper, zest, and lime juice. Add the chicken breasts and coat well. Cover and marinate in the refrigerator for 30 minutes.

2. Insert the Grill Grate and close the hood. Select GRILL, set the temperature to MEDIUM, and set the time to 18 minutes. Select START/STOP to begin preheating.

3. When the unit has beeped to signify it has preheated, place the chicken breasts on the Grill Grate. Close the hood and GRILL for 7 minutes. After 7 minutes, flip the chicken, close the hood, and GRILL for an additional 7 minutes.

4. Check the chicken for doneness. If needed, GRILL up to 4 minutes more. Cooking is complete when the internal temperature of the chicken reaches at least 165°F on a food thermometer.

5. Remove from the grill, and place on a cutting board or platter to rest for 5inutes. Serve.

Maple-teriyaki Chicken Wings

Servings: 4
Cooking Time: 14 Minutes
Ingredients:

- 1 cup maple syrup
- ⅓ cup soy sauce
- ¼ cup teriyaki sauce
- 3 garlic cloves, minced
- 2 teaspoons garlic powder
- 2 teaspoons onion powder
- 1 teaspoon freshly ground black pepper
- 2 pounds bone-in chicken wings (drumettes and flats)

Directions:

1. Insert the Grill Grate and close the hood. Select GRILL, set the temperature to MEDIUM, and set the time to 14 minutes. Select START/STOP to begin preheating.
2. Meanwhile, in a large bowl, whisk together the maple syrup, soy sauce, teriyaki sauce, garlic, garlic powder, onion powder, and black pepper. Add the wings, and use tongs to toss and coat.
3. When the unit has beeped to signify it has preheated, place the chicken wings on the Grill Grate. Close the hood and GRILL for 5 minutes. After 5 minutes, flip the wings, close the hood, and GRILL for an additional 5 minutes.
4. Check the wings for doneness. Cooking is complete when the internal temperature of the meat reaches at least 165°F on a food thermometer. If needed, GRILL for up to 4 minutes more.
5. Remove from the grill and serve.

Orange And Honey Glazed Duck With Apples

Servings: 2 To 3
Cooking Time: 15 Minutes
Ingredients:

- 1 pound duck breasts
- Kosher salt and pepper, to taste
- Juice and zest of 1 orange
- ¼ cup honey
- 2 sprigs thyme, plus more for garnish
- 2 firm tart apples, such as Fuji

Directions:

1. Insert the Crisper Basket and close the hood. Select ROAST, set the temperature to 400°F, and set the time to 13 minutes. Select START/STOP to begin preheating.
2. Pat the duck breasts dry and, using a sharp knife, make 3 to 4 shallow, diagonal slashes in the skin. Turn the breasts and score the skin on the diagonal in the opposite direction to create a cross-hatch pattern. Season well with salt and pepper.
3. Place the duck breasts skin-side up in the Crisper Basket. Close the hood and ROAST for 8 minutes. Flip and roast for 4 more minutes on the second side.
4. While the duck is roasting, prepare the sauce. Combine the orange juice and zest, honey, and thyme in a small saucepan. Bring to a boil, stirring to dissolve the honey, then reduce the heat and simmer until thickened. Core the apples and cut into quarters. Cut each quarter into 3 or 4 slices depending on the size.
5. After the duck has cooked on both sides, turn it and brush the skin with the orange-honey glaze. Roast for 1 more minute. Remove the duck breasts to a cutting board and allow to rest.
6. Toss the apple slices with the remaining orange-honey sauce in a medium bowl. Arrange the apples in a single layer in the Crisper Basket. AIR CRISP for 10 minutes while the duck breast rests. Slice the duck breasts on the bias and divide them and the apples among 2 or 3 plates.
7. Serve warm, garnished with additional thyme.

Turkey Meatballs With Cranberry Sauce

Servings: 4
Cooking Time: 20 Minutes

Ingredients:

- 2 tablespoons onion powder
- 1 cup plain bread crumbs
- 2 large eggs
- 2 tablespoons light brown sugar, packed
- 1 tablespoon salt
- 2 pounds ground turkey
- 1 (14-ounce) can cranberry sauce

Directions:

1. In a large bowl, mix together the onion powder, bread crumbs, eggs, brown sugar, and salt. Place the ground turkey in the bowl. Using your hands, mix the ingredients together just until combined (overmixing can make the meat tough and chewy). Form the mixture into 1½- to 2-inch meatballs. This should make 20 to 22 meatballs.
2. Insert the Grill Grate and close the hood. Select GRILL, set the temperature to MED, and set the time to 20 minutes. Select START/STOP to begin preheating.
3. When the unit beeps to signify it has preheated, place the meatballs on the Grill Grate. Close the hood and cook for 10 minutes.
4. After 10 minutes, open the hood and flip the meatballs. Close the hood and cook for 10 minutes more.
5. When cooking is complete, remove the meatballs from the grill. Place the cranberry sauce in a small bowl and use a whisk to stir it into more of a thick jelly sauce. Serve the meatballs with the sauce on the side.

Crispy Chicken Strips

Servings: 4
Cooking Time: 20 Minutes

Ingredients:

- 1 tablespoon olive oil
- 1 pound boneless, skinless chicken tenderloins
- 1 teaspoon salt
- ½ teaspoon freshly ground black pepper
- ½ teaspoon paprika
- ½ teaspoon garlic powder
- ½ cup whole-wheat seasoned bread crumbs
- 1 teaspoon dried parsley
- Cooking spray

Directions:

1. Spray the Crisper Basket lightly with cooking spray.
2. Insert the Crisper Basket and close the hood. Select AIR CRISP, set the temperature to 370°F, and set the time to 20 minutes. Select START/STOP to begin preheating.
3. In a medium bowl, toss the chicken with the salt, pepper, paprika, and garlic powder until evenly coated.
4. Add the olive oil and toss to coat the chicken evenly.
5. In a separate, shallow bowl, mix together the bread crumbs and parsley.
6. Coat each piece of chicken evenly in the bread crumb mixture.
7. Place the chicken in the Crisper Basket in a single layer and spray it lightly with cooking spray. You may need to cook them in batches.
8. Close the hood and AIR CRISP for 10 minutes. Flip the chicken over, lightly spray it with cooking spray, and AIR CRISP for an additional 8 to 10 minutes, until golden brown. Serve.

Herbed Grilled Chicken Thighs

Servings: 4
Cooking Time: 13 Minutes
Ingredients:

- Grated zest of 2 lemons
- Juice of 2 lemons
- 3 sprigs fresh rosemary, leaves finely chopped
- 3 sprigs fresh sage, leaves finely chopped
- 2 garlic cloves, minced
- ¼ teaspoon red pepper flakes
- ¼ cup canola oil
- Sea salt
- 4 boneless chicken thighs

Directions:

1. In a small bowl, whisk together the lemon zest and juice, rosemary, sage, garlic, red pepper flakes, and oil. Season with salt.

2. Place the chicken and lemon-herb mixture in a large resealable plastic bag or container. Toss to coat evenly. Refrigerate the chicken for at least 30 minutes.

3. Insert the Grill Grate and close the hood. Select GRILL, set the temperature to HIGH, and set the time to 13 minutes. Select START/STOP to begin preheating.

4. When the unit beeps to signify it has preheated, place the chicken on the Grill Grate. Close the hood and GRILL for 10 to 13 minutes.

5. Cooking is complete when the internal temperature of the chicken reaches at least 165°F on a food thermometer.

Spicy Chicken Kebabs

Servings: 4
Cooking Time: 14 Minutes
Ingredients:

- 1 tablespoon ground cumin
- 1 tablespoon garlic powder
- 1 tablespoon chili powder
- 2 teaspoons paprika
- ¼ teaspoon sea salt
- ¼ teaspoon freshly ground black pepper
- 1 pound boneless, skinless chicken breasts, cut in 2-inch cubes
- 2 tablespoons extra-virgin olive oil, divided
- 2 red bell peppers, seeded and cut into 1-inch cubes
- 1 red onion, quartered
- Juice of 1 lime

Directions:

1. In a small mixing bowl, combine the cumin, garlic powder, chili powder, paprika, salt, and pepper, and mix well.

2. Place the chicken, 1 tablespoon oil, and half of the spice mixture into a large resealable plastic bag or container. Toss to coat evenly.

3. Place the bell pepper, onion, remaining 1 tablespoon of oil, and remaining spice mixture into a large resealable plastic bag or container. Toss to coat evenly. Refrigerate the chicken and vegetables for at least 30 minutes.

4. Insert the Grill Grate and close the hood. Select GRILL, set the temperature to HIGH, and set the time to 14 minutes. Select START/STOP to begin preheating.

5. While the unit is preheating, assemble the kebabs by threading the chicken onto the wood skewers, alternating with the peppers and onion. Ensure the ingredients are pushed almost completely down to the end of the skewers.

6. When the unit beeps to signify it has preheated, place the skewers on the Grill Grate. Close the hood and GRILL for 10 to 14 minutes.

7. Cooking is complete when the internal temperature of the chicken reaches 165°F. When cooking is complete, remove from the heat, and drizzle with lime juice.

Spiced Breaded Chicken Cutlets

Servings: 2
Cooking Time: 11 Minutes
Ingredients:

- ½ pound boneless, skinless chicken breasts, horizontally sliced in half, into cutlets
- ½ tablespoon extra-virgin olive oil
- ⅛ cup bread crumbs
- ¼ teaspoon sea salt
- ¼ teaspoon freshly ground black pepper
- ¼ teaspoon paprika
- ¼ teaspoon garlic powder
- ⅛ teaspoon onion powder

Directions:
1. Insert the Crisper Basket and close the hood. Select AIR CRISP, set the temperature to 375°F, and set the time to 11 minutes. Select START/STOP to begin preheating.
2. Brush each side of the chicken cutlets with the oil.
3. Combine the bread crumbs, salt, pepper, paprika, garlic powder, and onion powder in a medium shallow bowl. Dredge the chicken cutlets in the bread crumb mixture, turning several times, to ensure the chicken is fully coated.
4. When the unit beeps to signify it has preheated, place the chicken in the basket. Close the hood and AIR CRISP for 9 minutes. Cooking is complete when the internal temperature of the meat reaches at least 165°F on a food thermometer. If needed, AIR CRISP for up to 2 minutes more.
5. Remove the chicken cutlets and serve immediately.

Honey Rosemary Chicken

Servings: 4
Cooking Time: 20 Minutes
Ingredients:

- ¼ cup balsamic vinegar
- ¼ cup honey
- 2 tablespoons olive oil
- 1 tablespoon dried rosemary leaves
- 1 teaspoon salt
- ½ teaspoon freshly ground black pepper
- 2 whole boneless, skinless chicken breasts, halved
- Cooking spray

Directions:
1. In a large resealable bag, combine the vinegar, honey, olive oil, rosemary, salt, and pepper. Add the chicken pieces, seal the bag, and refrigerate to marinate for at least 2 hours.
2. Insert the Crisper Basket and close the hood. Select BAKE, set the temperature to 325°F, and set the time to 20 minutes. Select START/STOP to begin preheating.
3. Line the Crisper Basket with parchment paper.
4. Remove the chicken from the marinade and place it on the parchment. Spritz with cooking spray.
5. Close the hood and BAKE for 10 minutes. Flip the chicken, spritz it with cooking spray, and bake for 10 minutes more until the internal temperature reaches 165°F and the chicken is no longer pink inside. Let sit for 5 minutes before serving.

Simple Whole Chicken Bake

Servings: 2 To 4
Cooking Time: 1 Hour
Ingredients:

- ½ cup melted butter
- 3 tablespoons garlic, minced
- Salt, to taste
- 1 teaspoon ground black pepper
- 1 whole chicken

Directions:
1. Select BAKE, set the temperature to 350°F, and set the time to 1 hour. Select START/STOP to begin preheating.
2. Combine the butter with garlic, salt, and ground black pepper in a small bowl.
3. Brush the butter mixture over the whole chicken, then place the chicken in a baking pan, skin side down.
4. Place the pan directly in the pot. Close the hood and BAKE for 1 hour, or until an instant-read thermometer inserted in the thickest part of the chicken registers at least 165°F. Flip the chicken halfway through.
5. Remove the chicken from the grill and allow to cool for 15 minutes before serving.

Fried Chicken Piccata

Servings: 2
Cooking Time: 22 Minutes
Ingredients:

- 2 large eggs
- ½ cup all-purpose flour
- ½ teaspoon freshly ground black pepper
- 2 boneless, skinless chicken breasts
- 4 tablespoons unsalted butter
- Juice of 1 lemon
- 1 tablespoon capers, drained

Directions:

1. Insert the Crisper Basket and close the hood. Select AIR CRISP, set the temperature to 375°F, and set the time to 22 minutes. Select START/STOP to begin preheating.
2. Meanwhile, in a medium shallow bowl, whisk the eggs until they are fully beaten.
3. In a separate medium shallow bowl, combine the flour and black pepper, using a fork to distribute the pepper evenly throughout.
4. Dredge the chicken in the flour to coat it completely, then dip it into the egg, then back in the flour.
5. When the unit beeps to signify it has preheated, place the chicken in the basket. Close the hood and AIR CRISP for 18 minutes.
6. While the chicken is cooking, melt the butter in a skillet over medium heat. Add the lemon juice and capers, and bring to a simmer. Reduce the heat to low, and simmer for 4 minutes.
7. After 18 minutes, check the chicken. Cooking is complete when the internal temperature of the meat reaches at least 165°F on a food thermometer. If necessary, close the hood and continue cooking for up to 3 minutes more.
8. Plate the chicken, and drizzle the butter sauce over each serving.

Lemon And Rosemary Chicken

Servings: 4
Cooking Time: 15 Minutes
Ingredients:

- 3 pounds bone-in, skin-on chicken thighs
- 4 tablespoons avocado oil
- 2 tablespoons lemon-pepper seasoning
- 1 tablespoon chopped fresh rosemary
- 1 lemon, thinly sliced

Directions:

1. Insert the Grill Grate and close the hood. Select GRILL, set the temperature to LO, and set the time to 15 minutes. Select START/STOP to begin preheating.
2. Coat the chicken thighs with the avocado oil and rub the lemon-pepper seasoning and rosemary evenly over the chicken.
3. When the unit beeps to signify it has preheated, place the chicken thighs on the Grill Grate, skin-side up. Place the lemon slices on top of the chicken. Close the hood and grill for 8 minutes.
4. After 8 minutes, open the hood and remove the lemon slices. Flip the chicken and place the lemon slices back on top. Close the hood and cook for 7 minutes more.
5. When cooking is complete, remove the chicken from the grill and serve.

Seafood Recipes

Tomato-stuffed Grilled Sole

Servings: 6
Cooking Time: 7 Minutes
Ingredients:

- 6 tablespoons mayonnaise
- 1 teaspoon garlic powder
- 1 (14-ounce) can diced tomatoes, drained
- 6 (4-ounce) sole fillets
- Cooking spray
- 6 tablespoons panko bread crumbs

Directions:

1. Insert the Grill Grate and close the hood. Select GRILL, set the temperature to HI, and set the time to 7 minutes. Select START/STOP to begin preheating.

2. While the unit is preheating, in a small bowl, combine the mayonnaise and garlic powder. Slowly fold in the tomatoes, making sure to be gentle so they don't turn to mush. Place the sole fillets on a large, flat surface and spread the mayonnaise across the top of each. Roll up the fillets, creating pinwheels. Spray the top of each roll with cooking spray, then press 1 tablespoon of panko bread crumbs on top of each.

3. When the unit beeps to signify it has preheated, place the fillets on the Grill Grate, seam-side down. Close the hood and grill for 7 minutes.

4. When cooking is complete, the panko bread crumbs will be crisp, and the fish will have turned opaque. Remove the fish from the grill and serve.

Orange-ginger Soy Salmon

Servings: 4
Cooking Time: 12 Minutes
Ingredients:

- ½ cup low-sodium soy sauce
- ¼ cup orange marmalade
- 3 tablespoons light brown sugar, packed
- 1 tablespoon peeled minced fresh ginger
- 1 garlic clove, minced
- 4 (8-ounce) skin-on salmon fillets

Directions:

1. In a large bowl, whisk together the soy sauce, orange marmalade, brown sugar, ginger, and garlic until the sugar is dissolved. Set aside one-quarter of the marinade in a small bowl. Place the salmon fillets skin-side down in the marinade in the large bowl.

2. Insert the Grill Grate and close the hood. Select GRILL, set the temperature to MED, and set the time to 12 minutes. Select START/STOP to begin preheating.

3. When the unit beeps to signify it has preheated, place the salmon fillets on the Grill Grate, skin-side down. Spoon the remaining marinade in the large bowl over the fillets. Close the hood and cook for 10 minutes.

4. After 10 minutes, open the hood and brush the reserved marinade in the small bowl over the fillets. Close the hood and cook for 2 minutes more.

5. When cooking is complete, the salmon will be opaque and should flake easily with a fork. (If you want, you can also use the Smart Thermometer at the end of cooking to check that the internal temperature of the salmon has reached 145°F.) Remove the fillets from the grill and serve.

Shrimp Boil

Servings: 6
Cooking Time: 10 Minutes
Ingredients:

- 2 tablespoons lemon-pepper seasoning
- 2 tablespoons light brown sugar, packed
- 2 tablespoons minced garlic
- 2 tablespoons Old Bay seasoning
- ¼ teaspoon Cajun seasoning
- ¼ teaspoon paprika
- ¼ teaspoon cayenne pepper
- 1 teaspoon garlic powder
- 1½ cups (3 sticks) unsalted butter, cut into quarters
- 2 pounds shrimp

Directions:

1. Insert the Cooking Pot and close the hood. Select GRILL, set the temperature to MED, and set the time to 10 minutes. Select START/STOP to begin preheating.

2. While the unit is preheating, in a small bowl, combine the lemon pepper, brown sugar, minced garlic, Old Bay seasoning, Cajun seasoning, paprika, cayenne pepper, and garlic powder.

3. When the unit beeps to signify it has preheated, place the butter and the lemon-pepper mixture in the Cooking Pot. Insert the Grill Grate and place the shrimp on it in a single layer. Close the hood and grill for 5 minutes.

4. After 5 minutes, open the hood and use grill mitts to remove the Grill Grate. Place the shrimp in the Cooking Pot. Stir to combine. Close the hood and cook for 5 minutes more.

5. When cooking is complete, open the hood and stir once more. Then close the hood and let the butter set with the shrimp for 5 minutes. Serve.

Honey-walnut Shrimp

Servings: 4
Cooking Time: 8 Minutes
Ingredients:

- 2 ounces walnuts
- 2 tablespoons honey
- 1 egg
- 1 cup panko bread crumbs
- 1 pound shrimp, peeled
- ½ cup mayonnaise
- 1 teaspoon powdered sugar
- 2 tablespoons heavy (whipping) cream
- Scallions, both white and green parts, sliced, for garnish

Directions:

1. Insert the Grill Grate. In a small heat-safe bowl, combine the walnuts and honey, then place the bowl on the Grill Grate and close the hood. Select GRILL, set the temperature to HI, and set the time to 8 minutes. Select START/STOP to begin preheating. After 2 minutes of preheating (set a separate timer), remove the bowl. Close the hood to continue preheating.

2. While the unit is preheating, create an assembly line with 2 large bowls. In the first bowl, whisk the egg. Put the panko bread crumbs in the other bowl. One at a time, dip the shrimp in the egg and then into the panko bread crumbs until well coated. Place the breaded shrimp on a plate.

3. When the unit beeps to signify it has preheated, place the shrimp on the Grill Grate in a single layer. Close the hood and cook for 4 minutes.

4. After 4 minutes, open the hood and flip the shrimp. Close the hood and cook for 4 minutes more.

5. While the shrimp are cooking, in a large bowl, combine the mayonnaise, powdered sugar, and heavy cream and mix until the sugar has dissolved.

6. When cooking is complete, remove the shrimp from the grill. Add the cooked shrimp and honey walnuts to the mayonnaise mixture and gently fold them together. Garnish with scallions and serve.

Mom's Lemon-pepper Salmon

Servings: 4
Cooking Time: 8 Minutes
Ingredients:

- ¼ cup mayonnaise
- 4 (4- to 5-ounce) skin-on salmon fillets
- 1 tablespoon lemon-pepper seasoning

Directions:

1. Insert the Grill Grate and close the hood. Select GRILL, set the temperature to MED, and set the time to 8 minutes. Select START/STOP to begin preheating.
2. While the unit is preheating, spread the mayonnaise evenly on the flesh of each salmon fillet. Season with the lemon pepper.
3. When the unit beeps to signify it has preheated, place the fillets on the Grill Grate, skin-side down. Close the hood and cook for 8 minutes.
4. When cooking is complete, the salmon will be opaque and should flake easily with a fork. (If you want, you can also use the Smart Thermometer at the end of cooking to check that the internal temperature of the salmon has reached 145°F.) Remove the salmon from the grill and serve.

Coconut Shrimp With Orange Chili Sauce

Servings:44
Cooking Time: 16 Minutes
Ingredients:

- For the coconut shrimp
- 2 large eggs
- 1 cup sweetened coconut flakes
- 1 cup panko bread crumbs
- ½ teaspoon salt
- ¼ teaspoon freshly ground black pepper
- 2 pounds jumbo shrimp, peeled
- For the orange chili sauce
- ½ cup orange marmalade
- 1 teaspoon sriracha or ¼ teaspoon red pepper flakes

Directions:

1. Insert the Grill Grate and close the hood. Select GRILL, set the temperature to HI, and set the time to 16 minutes. Select START/STOP to begin preheating.
2. While the unit is preheating, create an assembly line with 2 large bowls. In one bowl, whisk the eggs. In the other bowl, combine the coconut flakes, panko bread crumbs, salt, and pepper. One at a time, dip the shrimp in the egg and then into the coconut flakes until fully coated.
3. When the unit beeps to signify it has preheated, place half the shrimp on the Grill Grate in a single layer. Close the hood and cook for 4 minutes.
4. After 4 minutes, open the hood and flip the shrimp. Close the hood and cook for 4 minutes more. After 4 minutes, open the hood and remove the shrimp from the grill.
5. Repeat steps 3 and 4 for the remaining shrimp.
6. To make the orange chili sauce
7. In a small bowl, combine the orange marmalade and sriracha. Serve as a dipping sauce alongside the coconut shrimp.

Chili-lime Shrimp Skewers

Servings: 4
Cooking Time: 10 Minutes
Ingredients:

- 2 pounds jumbo shrimp, peeled
- 1 tablespoon chili powder
- ¼ teaspoon ground cumin
- ¼ teaspoon dried oregano
- ¼ teaspoon garlic powder
- 2 tablespoons honey
- Juice of 2 limes, divided
- Instant rice, prepared as directed

Directions:

1. Insert the Grill Grate and close the hood. Select GRILL, set the temperature to HI, and set the time to 5 minutes. Select START/STOP to begin preheating.
2. While the unit is preheating, thread 4 or 5 shrimp onto each of 8 skewers, leaving about an inch of space at the bottom. Place the skewers on a large plate.
3. In a small bowl, combine the chili powder, cumin, oregano, and garlic powder. Lightly coat the shrimp with the dry rub. In the same bowl, add the honey and the juice of ½ lime to any remaining seasoning. Mix together.
4. When the unit beeps to signify it has preheated, place 4 shrimp skewers on the Grill Grate. Brush the shrimp with some of the honey mixture. Close the hood and grill for 2 minutes, 30 seconds.
5. After 2 minutes, 30 seconds, open the hood and squeeze the juice of another ½ lime over the skewers and flip. Brush on more honey mixture. Close the hood and cook for 2 minutes, 30 seconds.
6. When cooking is complete, the shrimp should be opaque and pink. Remove the skewers from the grill. Select GRILL, set the temperature to HI, and set the time to 5 minutes. Select START/STOP to begin and press PREHEAT to skip preheating. Repeat steps 4 and 5 for the remaining 4 skewers. When all of the skewers are cooked, serve with the rice.

Lemon-garlic Butter Scallops

Servings: 6
Cooking Time: 4 Minutes
Ingredients:

- 2 pounds large sea scallops
- Salt
- Freshly ground black pepper
- 3 tablespoons avocado oil
- 3 garlic cloves, minced
- 8 tablespoons (1 stick) unsalted butter, sliced
- Juice of 1 lemon
- Chopped fresh parsley, for garnish

Directions:

1. Insert the Cooking Pot and close the hood. Select GRILL, set the temperature to HI, and set the time to 4 minutes. Select START/STOP to begin preheating.
2. While the unit is preheating, pat the scallops dry with a paper towel and season them with salt and pepper. After 5 minutes of preheating (set a separate timer), open the hood and add the avocado oil and garlic to the Cooking Pot, then close the hood to continue preheating.
3. When the unit beeps to signify it has preheated, use a spatula to spread the oil and garlic around the bottom of the Cooking Pot. Place the scallops in the pot in a single layer. Close the hood and cook for 2 minutes.
4. After 2 minutes, open the hood and flip the scallops. Add the butter to the pot and drizzle some lemon juice over each scallop. Close the hood and cook for 2 minutes more.
5. When cooking is complete, open the hood and flip the scallops again. Spoon melted garlic butter on top of each. The scallops should be slightly firm and opaque. Remove the scallops from the grill and serve, garnished with the parsley.

Desserts Recipes

Blackberry Chocolate Cake

Servings: 8
Cooking Time: 22 Minutes
Ingredients:

- ½ cup butter, at room temperature
- 2 ounces Swerve
- 4 eggs
- 1 cup almond flour
- 1 teaspoon baking soda
- ⅓ teaspoon baking powder
- ½ cup cocoa powder
- 1 teaspoon orange zest
- ⅓ cup fresh blackberries

Directions:

1. Select BAKE, set the temperature to 335°F, and set the time to 22 minutes. Select START/STOP to begin preheating.
2. With an electric mixer or hand mixer, beat the butter and Swerve until creamy.
3. One at a time, mix in the eggs and beat again until fluffy.
4. Add the almond flour, baking soda, baking powder, cocoa powder, orange zest and mix well. Add the butter mixture to the almond flour mixture and stir until well blended. Fold in the blackberries.
5. Scrape the batter to a baking pan. Place the pan directly in the pot. Close the hood and BAKE for 22 minutes. Check the cake for doneness: If a toothpick inserted into the center of the cake comes out clean, it's done.
6. Allow the cake cool on a wire rack to room temperature. Serve immediately.

Simple Corn Biscuits

Servings: 6
Cooking Time: 15 Minutes
Ingredients:

- 1½ cups all-purpose flour, plus additional for dusting
- ½ cup yellow cornmeal
- 2½ teaspoons baking powder
- ½ teaspoon sea salt
- ⅓ cup vegetable shortening
- ⅔ cup buttermilk
- Nonstick cooking spray

Directions:

1. In a large bowl, combine the flour, cornmeal, baking powder, and salt.
2. Add the shortening, and cut it into the flour mixture, until well combined and the dough resembles a coarse meal. Add the buttermilk and stir together just until moistened.
3. Insert the Crisper Basket and close the hood. Select AIR CRISP, set the temperature to 350°F, and set the time to 15 minutes. Select START/STOP to begin preheating.
4. While the unit is preheating, dust a clean work surface with flour. Knead the mixture on the floured surface until a cohesive dough forms. Roll out the dough to an even thickness, then cut into biscuits with a 2-inch biscuit cutter.
5. When the unit beeps to signify it has preheated, coat the basket with cooking spray. Place 6 to 8 biscuits in the basket, well spaced, and spray each with cooking spray. Close the hood and AIR CRISP for 12 to 15 minutes, until golden brown.
6. Gently remove the biscuits from the basket, and place them on a wire rack to cool. Repeat with the remaining dough.

Chia Pudding

Servings: 2
Cooking Time: 4 Minutes
Ingredients:

- 1 cup chia seeds
- 1 cup unsweetened coconut milk
- 1 teaspoon liquid stevia
- 1 tablespoon coconut oil
- 1 teaspoon butter, melted

Directions:

1. Select BAKE, set the temperature to 360ºF, and set the time to 4 minutes. Select START/STOP to begin preheating.
2. Mix together the chia seeds, coconut milk, and stevia in a large bowl. Add the coconut oil and melted butter and stir until well blended.
3. Divide the mixture evenly between the ramekins, filling only about ⅔ of the way. Transfer to the pot.
4. Close the hood and BAKE for 4 minutes.
5. Allow to cool for 5 minutes and serve warm.

Pear And Apple Crisp

Servings: 6
Cooking Time: 20 Minutes
Ingredients:

- ½ pound apples, cored and chopped
- ½ pound pears, cored and chopped
- 1 cup flour
- 1 cup sugar
- 1 tablespoon butter
- 1 teaspoon ground cinnamon
- ¼ teaspoon ground cloves
- 1 teaspoon vanilla extract
- ¼ cup chopped walnuts
- Whipped cream, for serving

Directions:

1. Select BAKE, set the temperature to 340ºF, and set the time to 20 minutes. Select START/STOP to begin preheating.
2. Lightly grease a baking pan and place the apples and pears inside.
3. Combine the rest of the ingredients, minus the walnuts and the whipped cream, until a coarse, crumbly texture is achieved.
4. Pour the mixture over the fruits and spread it evenly. Top with the chopped walnuts.
5. Place the pan directly in the pot. Close the hood and BAKE for 20 minutes or until the top turns golden brown.
6. Serve at room temperature with whipped cream.

Classic Pound Cake

Servings: 8
Cooking Time: 30 Minutes
Ingredients:

- 1 stick butter, at room temperature
- 1 cup Swerve
- 4 eggs
- 1½ cups coconut flour
- ½ cup buttermilk
- ½ teaspoon baking soda
- ½ teaspoon baking powder
- ¼ teaspoon salt
- 1 teaspoon vanilla essence
- A pinch of ground star anise
- A pinch of freshly grated nutmeg
- Cooking spray

Directions:

1. Select BAKE, set the temperature to 320ºF, and set the time to 30 minutes. Select START/STOP to begin preheating.
2. Spray a baking pan with cooking spray.
3. With an electric mixer or hand mixer, beat the butter and Swerve until creamy. One at a time, mix in the eggs and whisk until fluffy. Add the remaining ingredients and stir to combine.
4. Transfer the batter to the prepared baking pan. Place the pan directly in the pot. Close the hood and BAKE for 30 minutes until the center of the cake is springy. Rotate the pan halfway through the cooking time.
5. Allow the cake to cool in the pan for 10 minutes before removing and serving.

Grilled Apple Fries With Caramel Cream Cheese Dip

Servings: 4
Cooking Time: 5 Minutes
Ingredients:

- 4 apples, such as Honeycrisp, Gala, Pink Lady, or Granny Smith, peeled, cored, and sliced
- ¼ cup heavy (whipping) cream
- 1 tablespoon granulated sugar
- ¼ teaspoon cinnamon
- ¼ cup all-purpose flour
- 4 ounces cream cheese, at room temperature
- 1 tablespoon caramel sauce
- 1 tablespoon light brown sugar, packed

Directions:

1. Insert the Grill Grate and close the hood. Select GRILL, set the temperature to MAX, and set the time to 5 minutes. Select START/STOP to begin preheating.
2. In a large bowl, toss the apple slices with the heavy cream, granulated sugar, and cinnamon to coat. Slowly shake in the flour and continue mixing to coat.
3. In a small bowl, mix together the cream cheese, caramel sauce, and brown sugar until smooth. Set aside.
4. When the unit beeps to signify it has preheated, place the apples on the Grill Grate in a single layer. Close the hood and grill for 2 minutes, 30 seconds.
5. After 2 minutes, 30 seconds, open the hood and flip and toss the apples around. Close the hood and cook for 2 minutes, 30 seconds more.
6. When cooking is complete, open the hood and remove the apple chips from the grill. Serve with the sauce.

Orange Cake

Servings: 8
Cooking Time: 23 Minutes
Ingredients:

- Nonstick baking spray with flour
- 1¼ cups all-purpose flour
- ⅓ cup yellow cornmeal
- ¾ cup white sugar
- 1 teaspoon baking soda
- ¼ cup safflower oil
- 1¼ cups orange juice, divided
- 1 teaspoon vanilla
- ¼ cup powdered sugar

Directions:

1. Select BAKE, set the temperature to 350°F, and set the time to 23 minutes. Select START/STOP to begin preheating.
2. Spray a baking pan with nonstick spray and set aside.
3. In a medium bowl, combine the flour, cornmeal, sugar, baking soda, safflower oil, 1 cup of the orange juice, and vanilla, and mix well.
4. Pour the batter into the baking pan. Place the pan directly in the pot. Close the hood and BAKE for 23 minutes or until a toothpick inserted in the center of the cake comes out clean.
5. Remove the cake from the grill and place on a cooling rack. Using a toothpick, make about 20 holes in the cake.
6. In a small bowl, combine remaining ¼ cup of orange juice and the powdered sugar and stir well. Drizzle this mixture over the hot cake slowly so the cake absorbs it.
7. Cool completely, then cut into wedges to serve.

Grilled Strawberry Pound Cake

Servings: 8

Cooking Time: 8 Minutes

Ingredients:

- 1 loaf pound cake, cut into ¼-inch-thick slices (8 slices)
- 4 tablespoons (½ stick) unsalted butter, melted
- 2 cups strawberries, sliced
- 1 tablespoon granulated sugar
- Juice of ¼ lemon

Directions:

1. Insert the Grill Grate and close the hood. Select GRILL, set the temperature to HI, and set the time to 8 minutes. Select START/STOP to begin preheating.

2. While the unit is preheating, brush both sides of the pound cake slices with the melted butter. In a small bowl, combine the strawberries, sugar, and lemon juice.

3. When the unit beeps to signify it has preheated, place 4 slices of pound cake on the Grill Grate. Close the hood and grill for 2 minutes.

4. After 2 minutes, open the hood and flip the pound cake slices. Top each with ¼ cup of strawberries. Close the hood and cook for 2 minutes.

5. After 2 minutes, open the hood and carefully remove the grilled pound cake. Repeat steps 3 and 4 with the remaining pound cake and strawberries. Serve.

Coffee Chocolate Cake

Servings: 8

Cooking Time: 30 Minutes

Ingredients:

- Dry Ingredients:
- 1½ cups almond flour
- ½ cup coconut meal
- ⅔ cup Swerve
- 1 teaspoon baking powder
- ¼ teaspoon salt
- Wet Ingredients:
- 1 egg
- 1 stick butter, melted
- ½ cup hot strongly brewed coffee
- Topping:
- ½ cup confectioner's Swerve
- ¼ cup coconut flour
- 3 tablespoons coconut oil
- 1 teaspoon ground cinnamon
- ½ teaspoon ground cardamom

Directions:

1. Select BAKE, set the temperature to 330ºF, and set the time to 30 minutes. Select START/STOP to begin preheating.

2. In a medium bowl, combine the almond flour, coconut meal, Swerve, baking powder, and salt.

3. In a large bowl, whisk the egg, melted butter, and coffee until smooth.

4. Add the dry mixture to the wet and stir until well incorporated. Transfer the batter to a greased baking pan.

5. Stir together all the ingredients for the topping in a small bowl. Spread the topping over the batter and smooth the top with a spatula.

6. Place the pan directly in the pot. Close the hood and BAKE for 30 minutes, or until the cake springs back when gently pressed with your fingers.

7. Rest for 10 minutes before serving.

Chocolate And Peanut Butter Lava Cupcakes

Servings: 8
Cooking Time: 10 To 13 Minutes
Ingredients:

- Nonstick baking spray with flour
- 1⅓ cups chocolate cake mix
- 1 egg
- 1 egg yolk
- ¼ cup safflower oil
- ¼ cup hot water
- ⅓ cup sour cream
- 3 tablespoons peanut butter
- 1 tablespoon powdered sugar

Directions:

1. Select BAKE, set the temperature to 350°F, and set the time to 13 minutes. Select START/STOP to begin preheating.
2. Double up 16 foil muffin cups to make 8 cups. Spray each lightly with nonstick spray; set aside.
3. In a medium bowl, combine the cake mix, egg, egg yolk, safflower oil, water, and sour cream, and beat until combined.
4. In a small bowl, combine the peanut butter and powdered sugar and mix well. Form this mixture into 8 balls.
5. Spoon about ¼ cup of the chocolate batter into each muffin cup and top with a peanut butter ball. Spoon remaining batter on top of the peanut butter balls to cover them.
6. Arrange the cups in the pot, leaving some space between each. Place the pan directly in the pot. Close the hood and BAKE for 10 to 13 minutes or until the tops look dry and set.
7. Let the cupcakes cool for about 10 minutes, then serve warm.

Strawberry Pizza

Servings: 4
Cooking Time: 6 Minutes
Ingredients:

- 2 tablespoons all-purpose flour, plus more as needed
- ½ store-bought pizza dough
- 1 tablespoon canola oil
- 1 cup sliced fresh strawberries
- 1 tablespoon sugar
- ½ cup chocolate-hazelnut spread

Directions:

1. Insert the Grill Grate and close the hood. Select GRILL, set the temperature to MAX, and set the time to 6 minutes. Select START/STOP to begin preheating.
2. While the unit is preheating, dust a clean work surface with the flour. Place the dough on the floured surface, and roll it out to a 9-inch round of even thickness. Dust your rolling pin and work surface with additional flour, as needed, to ensure the dough does not stick.
3. Brush the surface of the rolled-out dough evenly with half the oil. Flip the dough over, and brush with the remaining oil. Poke the dough with a fork 5 or 6 times across its surface to prevent air pockets from forming during cooking.
4. When the unit beeps to signify it has preheated, place the dough on the Grill Grate. Close the hood and GRILL for 3 minutes.
5. After 3 minutes, flip the dough. Close the hood and continue grilling for the remaining 3 minutes.
6. Meanwhile, in a medium mixing bowl, combine the strawberries and sugar.
7. Transfer the pizza to a cutting board and let cool. Top with the chocolate-hazelnut spread and strawberries. Cut into pieces and serve.

Chocolate S'mores

Servings: 12
Cooking Time: 3 Minutes
Ingredients:

- 12 whole cinnamon graham crackers
- 2 chocolate bars, broken into 12 pieces
- 12 marshmallows

Directions:

1. Insert the Crisper Basket and close the hood. Select BAKE, set the temperature to 350°F, and set the time to 3 minutes. Select START/STOP to begin preheating.
2. Halve each graham cracker into 2 squares.
3. Put 6 graham cracker squares in the basket. Do not stack. Put a piece of chocolate into each. Close the hood and BAKE for 2 minutes.
4. Open the grill and add a marshmallow onto each piece of melted chocolate. Bake for 1 additional minute.
5. Remove the cooked s'mores from the grill, then repeat steps 2 and 3 for the remaining 6 s'mores.
6. Top with the remaining graham cracker squares and serve.

Chocolate Pecan Pie

Servings: 8
Cooking Time: 25 Minutes
Ingredients:

- 1 unbaked pie crust
- Filling:
- 2 large eggs
- ⅓ cup butter, melted
- 1 cup sugar
- ½ cup all-purpose flour
- 1 cup milk chocolate chips
- 1½ cups coarsely chopped pecans
- 2 tablespoons bourbon

Directions:

1. Select BAKE, set the temperature to 350°F, and set the time to 25 minutes. Select START/STOP to begin preheating.
2. Whisk the eggs and melted butter in a large bowl until creamy.
3. Add the sugar and flour and stir to incorporate. Mix in the milk chocolate chips, pecans, and bourbon and stir until well combined.
4. Use a fork to prick holes in the bottom and sides of the pie crust. Pour the prepared filling into the pie crust. Place the pie crust in the pot.
5. Close the hood and BAKE for 25 minutes until a toothpick inserted in the center comes out clean.
6. Allow the pie cool for 10 minutes in the basket before serving.

Easy Blackberry Cobbler

Servings: 6
Cooking Time: 25 To 30 Minutes
Ingredients:

- 3 cups fresh or frozen blackberries
- 1¾ cups sugar, divided
- 1 teaspoon vanilla extract
- 8 tablespoons butter, melted
- 1 cup self-rising flour
- Cooking spray

Directions:

1. Select BAKE, set the temperature to 350°F, and set the time to 30 minutes. Select START/STOP to begin preheating.
2. Spritz a baking pan with cooking spray.
3. Mix the blackberries, 1 cup of sugar, and vanilla in a medium bowl and stir to combine.
4. Stir together the melted butter, remaining sugar, and flour in a separate medium bowl.
5. Spread the blackberry mixture evenly in the prepared pan and top with the butter mixture.
6. Place the pan directly in the pot. Close the hood and BAKE for 20 to 25 minutes. Check for doneness and bake for another 5 minutes, if needed.
7. Remove from the grill and place on a wire rack to cool to room temperature. Serve immediately.

Grilled Banana S'mores

Servings: 4
Cooking Time: 6 Minutes
Ingredients:

- 4 large bananas
- 1 cup milk chocolate chips
- 1 cup mini marshmallows
- 4 graham crackers, crushed

Directions:

1. Insert the Cooking Pot and close the hood. Select GRILL, set the temperature to HI, and set the time to 6 minutes. Select START/STOP to begin preheating.

2. While the unit is preheating, prepare the banana boats. Starting at the bottom of a banana, slice the peel lengthwise up one side and then the opposite side. Pull the top half of the peel back, revealing the fruit underneath, but keeping the bottom of the banana peel intact. With a spoon, carefully scoop out some of the banana. (Eat it or set it aside.) Repeat with each banana. Equally divide the chocolate chips and marshmallows between the banana boats.

3. When the unit beeps to signify it has preheated, place the bananas in the Cooking Pot. Close the hood and cook for 6 minutes.

4. When cooking is complete, remove the bananas from the grill and sprinkle the crushed graham crackers on top. Serve.

Everyday Cheesecake

Servings: 4
Cooking Time: 35 Minutes
Ingredients:

- 1 large egg
- 8 ounces cream cheese, at room temperature
- ¼ cup heavy (whipping) cream
- ¼ cup sour cream
- ¼ cup powdered sugar
- 1 teaspoon vanilla extract
- 5 ounces cookies, such as chocolate, vanilla, cinnamon, or your favorite
- 4 tablespoons (½ stick) unsalted butter, melted

Directions:

1. In a large bowl, whisk the egg. Then add the cream cheese, heavy cream, and sour cream and whisk until smooth. Slowly add the powdered sugar and vanilla, whisking until fully mixed.

2. Insert the Cooking Pot and close the hood. Select BAKE, set the temperature to 350°F, and set the time to 35 minutes. Select START/STOP to begin preheating.

3. While the unit is preheating, crush the cookies into fine crumbs. Place them in a 6-inch springform pan and drizzle evenly with the melted butter. Using your fingers, press down on the crumbs to form a crust on the bottom of the pan. Pour the cream cheese mixture on top of the crust. Cover the pan with aluminum foil, making sure the foil fully covers the sides of the pan and tucks under the bottom so it does not lift up and block the Splatter Shield as the air flows while baking.

4. When the unit beeps to signify it has preheated, place the springform pan in the Cooking Pot. Close the hood and cook for 25 minutes.

5. After 25 minutes, open the hood and remove the foil. Close the hood and cook for 10 minutes more.

6. When cooking is complete, remove the pan from the Cooking Pot and let the cheesecake cool for 1 hour, then place the cheesecake in the refrigerator for at least 3 hours. Slice and serve.

Candied Pecans

Servings: 4

Cooking Time: 20 Minutes

Ingredients:

- 1 large egg white
- 1 teaspoon vanilla extract
- 1 tablespoon water
- ¼ cup granulated sugar
- ¼ cup light brown sugar, packed
- 1 teaspoon ground cinnamon
- 1 teaspoon salt
- 1 pound pecan halves

Directions:

1. Insert the Cooking Pot and close the hood. Select GRILL, set the temperature to MED, and set the time to 20 minutes. Select START/STOP to begin preheating.

2. While the unit is preheating, in a large bowl, whisk together the egg white, vanilla, and water until it becomes frothy.

3. In a small bowl, combine the granulated sugar, brown sugar, cinnamon, and salt. Add the pecans to the egg mixture, coating them well. Then add the sugar mixture and stir to coat the pecans evenly.

4. When the unit beeps to signify it has preheated, evenly spread the pecans in the Cooking Pot. Close the hood and grill for 5 minutes.

5. After 5 minutes, open the hood and stir the pecans. Close the hood and cook for 5 minutes. Repeat until the pecans have cooked for 20 minutes total.

6. When cooking is complete, remove the pecans from the Cooking Pot and spread them on a baking sheet to cool to room temperature. Store in a resealable bag or airtight container.

Peaches-and-cake Skewers

Servings: 4

Cooking Time: 8 Minutes

Ingredients:

- 1 loaf pound cake, cut into 1-inch cubes
- 4 peaches, sliced
- ½ cup condensed milk

Directions:

1. Insert the Grill Grate and close the hood. Select GRILL, set the temperature to HI, and set the time to 8 minutes. Select START/STOP to begin preheating.

2. While the unit is preheating, alternate cake cubes and peach slices, 3 or 4 pieces of each, on each of 12 skewers. Using a basting brush, brush the condensed milk onto the cake and peaches and place the skewers on a plate or baking sheet.

3. When the unit beeps to signify it has preheated, place 6 skewers on the Grill Grate. Close the hood and cook for 2 minutes.

4. After 2 minutes, open the hood and flip the skewers. Close the hood to cook for 2 minutes more.

5. After 2 minutes, open the hood and remove the skewers. Repeat steps 3 and 4 with the remaining 6 skewers. Serve.

Fudge Pie

Servings: 8
Cooking Time: 25 To 30 Minutes

Ingredients:

- 1½ cups sugar
- ½ cup self-rising flour
- ⅓ cup unsweetened cocoa powder
- 3 large eggs, beaten
- 12 tablespoons butter, melted
- 1½ teaspoons vanilla extract
- 1 unbaked pie crust
- ¼ cup confectioners' sugar (optional)

Directions:

1. Select BAKE, set the temperature to 350°F, and set the time to 30 minutes. Select START/STOP to begin preheating.
2. Thoroughly combine the sugar, flour, and cocoa powder in a medium bowl. Add the beaten eggs and butter and whisk to combine. Stir in the vanilla.
3. Pour the prepared filling into the pie crust and transfer to the pot.
4. Close the hood and BAKE for 25 to 30 minutes until just set.
5. Allow the pie to cool for 5 minutes. Sprinkle with the confectioners' sugar, if desired. Serve warm.

Churros With Chocolate-yogurt Sauce

Servings: 8
Cooking Time: 30 Minutes

Ingredients:

- 1 cup water
- 1 stick unsalted butter, cut into 8 pieces
- ½ cup sugar, plus 1 tablespoon
- 1 cup all-purpose flour
- 1 teaspoon vanilla extract
- 3 large eggs
- 2 teaspoons ground cinnamon
- Nonstick cooking spray
- 4 ounces dark chocolate, chopped
- ¼ cup Greek yogurt

Directions:

1. In a medium saucepan over medium-high heat, combine the water, butter, and the 1 tablespoon of sugar. Bring to a simmer. Add the flour, stirring it in quickly. Continue to cook, stirring constantly, until the mixture is thick, about 3 minutes. Transfer to a large bowl.
2. Using a spoon, beat the flour mixture for about 1 minute, until cooled slightly. Stir in the vanilla, then the eggs, one at a time.
3. Transfer the dough to a plastic bag or a piping bag. Let the dough rest for 1 hour at room temperature.
4. Insert the Crisper Basket and close the hood. Select AIR CRISP, set the temperature to 375°F, and set the time to 30 minutes. Select START/STOP to begin preheating.
5. Meanwhile, in a medium shallow bowl, combine the cinnamon and remaining ½ cup of sugar.
6. When the unit beeps to signify it has preheated, spray the basket with the nonstick cooking spray. Take the plastic bag with your dough and cut off one corner. Pipe the batter directly into the Crisper Basket, making 6 churros, placed at least ½ inch apart. Close the hood and AIR CRISP for 10 minutes.
7. Meanwhile, in a small microwave-safe mixing bowl, melt the chocolate in the microwave, stirring it after every 30 seconds, until completely melted and smooth. Add the yogurt and whisk until smooth.
8. After 10 minutes, carefully transfer the churros to the sugar mixture and toss to coat evenly. Repeat piping and air crisping with the remaining batter, adding time as needed.
9. Serve the churros with the warm chocolate dipping sauce.

Peanut Butter-chocolate Bread Pudding

Servings: 8
Cooking Time: 10 To 12 Minutes

Ingredients:

- 1 egg
- 1 egg yolk
- ¾ cup chocolate milk
- 3 tablespoons brown sugar
- 3 tablespoons peanut butter
- 2 tablespoons cocoa powder
- 1 teaspoon vanilla
- 5 slices firm white bread, cubed
- Nonstick cooking spray

Directions:

1. Select BAKE, set the temperature to 330ºF, and set the time to 12 minutes. Select START/STOP to begin preheating.
2. Spritz a baking pan with nonstick cooking spray.
3. Whisk together the egg, egg yolk, chocolate milk, brown sugar, peanut butter, cocoa powder, and vanilla until well combined.
4. Fold in the bread cubes and stir to mix well. Allow the bread soak for 10 minutes.
5. When ready, transfer the egg mixture to the prepared baking pan.
6. Place the pan directly in the pot. Close the hood and BAKE for 10 to 12 minutes, or until the pudding is just firm to the touch.
7. Serve at room temperature.

Curry Peaches, Pears, And Plums

Servings: 6 To 8
Cooking Time: 5 Minutes

Ingredients:

- 2 peaches
- 2 firm pears
- 2 plums
- 2 tablespoons melted butter
- 1 tablespoon honey
- 2 to 3 teaspoons curry powder

Directions:

1. Insert the Crisper Basket and close the hood. Select BAKE, set the temperature to 325ºF, and set the time to 8 minutes. Select START/STOP to begin preheating.
2. Cut the peaches in half, remove the pits, and cut each half in half again. Cut the pears in half, core them, and remove the stem. Cut each half in half again. Do the same with the plums.
3. Spread a large sheet of heavy-duty foil on the work surface. Arrange the fruit on the foil and drizzle with the butter and honey. Sprinkle with the curry powder.
4. Wrap the fruit in the foil, making sure to leave some air space in the packet.
5. Put the foil package in the basket. Close the hood and BAKE for 5 to 8 minutes, shaking the basket once during the cooking time, until the fruit is soft.
6. Serve immediately.

Rum Grilled Pineapple Sundaes

Servings: 6
Cooking Time: 8 Minutes
Ingredients:

- ½ cup dark rum
- ½ cup packed brown sugar
- 1 teaspoon ground cinnamon, plus more for garnish
- 1 pineapple, cored and sliced
- Vanilla ice cream, for serving

Directions:

1. In a large shallow bowl or storage container, combine the rum, sugar, and cinnamon. Add the pineapple slices and arrange them in a single layer. Coat with the mixture, then let soak for at least 5 minutes per side.
2. Insert the Grill Grate and close the hood. Select GRILL, set the temperature to MAX, and set the time to 8 minutes. Select START/STOP to begin preheating.
3. While the unit is preheating, strain the extra rum sauce from the pineapple.
4. When the unit beeps to signify it has preheated, place the fruit on the Grill Grate in a single layer (you may need to do this in multiple batches). Gently press the fruit down to maximize grill marks. Close the hood and GRILL for about 6 to 8 minutes without flipping. If working in batches, remove the pineapple, and repeat this step for the remaining pineapple slices.
5. When cooking is complete, remove, and top each pineapple ring with a scoop of ice cream. Sprinkle with cinnamon and serve immediately.

Ultimate Skillet Brownies

Servings: 6
Cooking Time: 40 Minutes
Ingredients:

- ½ cup all-purpose flour
- ¼ cup unsweetened cocoa powder
- ¾ teaspoon sea salt
- 2 large eggs
- 1 tablespoon water
- ½ cup granulated sugar
- ½ cup dark brown sugar
- 1 tablespoon vanilla extract
- 8 ounces semisweet chocolate chips, melted
- ¾ cup unsalted butter, melted
- Nonstick cooking spray

Directions:

1. In a medium bowl, whisk together the flour, cocoa powder, and salt.
2. In a large bowl, whisk together the eggs, water, sugar, brown sugar, and vanilla until smooth.
3. In a microwave-safe bowl, melt the chocolate in the microwave. In a separate microwave-safe bowl, melt the butter.
4. In a separate medium bowl, stir together the chocolate and butter until evenly combined. Whisk into the egg mixture. Then slowly add the dry ingredients, stirring just until incorporated.
5. Remove the Grill Grate from the unit. Select BAKE, set the temperature to 350°F, and set the time to 40 minutes. Select START/STOP to begin preheating.
6. Meanwhile, lightly grease the baking pan with cooking spray. Pour the batter into the pan, spreading evenly.
7. When the unit beeps to signify it has preheated, place the pan directly in the pot. Close the hood and BAKE for 40 minutes.
8. After 40 minutes, check that baking is complete. A wooden toothpick inserted into the center of the brownies should come out clean.

Cinnamon-sugar Dessert Chips

Servings: 4
Cooking Time: 10 Minutes
Ingredients:

- 10 (6-inch) flour tortillas
- 8 tablespoons (1 stick) unsalted butter, melted
- 1 tablespoon cinnamon
- ¼ cup granulated sugar
- ½ cup chocolate syrup, for dipping

Directions:

1. Insert the Grill Grate and close the hood. Select GRILL, set the temperature to HI, and set the time to 10 minutes. Select START/STOP to begin preheating.

2. While the unit is preheating, cut the tortillas into 6 equal wedges. In a large resealable bag, combine the tortillas, butter, cinnamon, and sugar and shake vigorously to coat the tortillas.

3. When the unit beeps to signify it has preheated, add half the tortillas to the Grill Grate. Close the hood and cook for 2 minutes, 30 seconds.

4. After 2 minutes, 30 seconds, open the hood and use a spatula to quickly flip the chips or move them around. Close the hood and cook for 2 minutes, 30 seconds more.

5. After 2 minutes, 30 seconds, open the hood and remove the grilled chips and repeat the process with the remaining tortillas.

6. Serve with the chocolate syrup for dipping.

Black And White Brownies

Servings:1
Cooking Time: 20 Minutes
Ingredients:

- 1 egg
- ¼ cup brown sugar
- 2 tablespoons white sugar
- 2 tablespoons safflower oil
- 1 teaspoon vanilla
- ⅓ cup all-purpose flour
- ¼ cup cocoa powder
- ¼ cup white chocolate chips
- Nonstick cooking spray

Directions:

1. Select BAKE, set the temperature to 340°F, and set the time to 20 minutes. Select START/STOP to begin preheating.

2. Spritz a baking pan with nonstick cooking spray.

3. Whisk together the egg, brown sugar, and white sugar in a medium bowl. Mix in the safflower oil and vanilla and stir to combine.

4. Add the flour and cocoa powder and stir just until incorporated. Fold in the white chocolate chips.

5. Scrape the batter into the prepared baking pan.

6. Place the pan directly in the pot. Close the hood and BAKE for 20 minutes, or until the brownie springs back when touched lightly with your fingers.

7. Transfer to a wire rack and let cool for 30 minutes before slicing to serve.

RECIPES INDEX

A

Apple-glazed Pork 51
Asparagus And Cheese Strata 19
Avocado Egg Rolls 37
Avocado Quesadillas 19

B

Baby Back Ribs In Gochujang Marinade 61
Bacon And Broccoli Bread Pudding 9
Bacon And Egg Bread Cups 22
Bacon Burger Meatballs 55
Bacon-wrapped Sausage With Tomato Relish 55
Balsamic Broccoli 41
Balsamic Dressing 48
Balsamic Honey Mustard Lamb Chops 59
Balsamic Mushroom Sliders With Pesto 30
Banana And Oat Bread Pudding 12
Banana Bread 20
Beef And Vegetable Cubes 60
Beef Stuffed Bell Peppers 36
Black And White Brownies 92
Blackberry Chocolate Cake 81
Blueberry Dump Cake 17
Breaded Green Olives 39
Breakfast Chilaquiles 16
Broccoli And Tofu Teriyaki 25
Brussels Sprouts And Bacon 44
Buttered Broccoli With Parmesan 28
Buttermilk Marinated Chicken Wings 45
Buttermilk Ranch Chicken Tenders 69

C

Candied Pecans 88
Carne Asada Tacos 64
Cauliflower Steaks With Ranch Dressing 29
Cayenne Sesame Nut Mix 38
Cheese And Ham Stuffed Baby Bella 45
Cheese And Spinach Stuffed Portobellos 26
Cheesy Apple Roll-ups 37
Cheesy Asparagus And Potato Platter 28
Cheesy Breakfast Casserole 22
Cheesy Broccoli Gratin 31
Cheesy Garlic Bread 46
Cheesy Jalapeño Popper Burgers 49
Cheesy Macaroni Balls 29
Cheesy Steak Fries 40
Chia Pudding 82
Chicken Breakfast Sausages 18
Chili-lime Shrimp Skewers 80
Chocolate And Peanut Butter Lava Cupcakes 85
Chocolate Banana Bread With White Chocolate 13
Chocolate Pecan Pie 86
Chocolate S'mores 86
Churros With Chocolate-yogurt Sauce 89
Cinnamon Sugar Roll-ups 8

Cinnamon Toast With Strawberries 10
Cinnamon-sugar Dessert Chips 92
Classic Pound Cake 82
Coconut Shrimp With Orange Chili Sauce 79
Coffee Chocolate Cake 84
Corn Pakodas 30
Cornflakes Toast Sticks 12
Country-fried Steak And Eggs 21
Crackling Pork Roast 59
Cream Cheese–stuffed French Toast 9
Crispy Chicken Strips 73
Crispy Cod Fingers 42
Crispy Pork Tenderloin 50
Crispy Spiced Potatoes 42
Crusted Brussels Sprouts With Sage 35
Crustless Broccoli Quiche 14
Curry Peaches, Pears, And Plums 90

D

Dill Chicken Strips 70

E

Easy Asian Turkey Meatballs 68
Easy Beef Schnitzel 50
Easy Blackberry Cobbler 86
Easy Muffuletta Sliders With Olives 43
Egg And Avocado Burrito 15
Eggplant Parmigiana 23
Everyday Cheesecake 87

F

Fast And Easy Asparagus 28
Fast Lamb Satay 60
Fluffy Pancake Sheet 18
French Fries 40
Fried Chicken Piccata 76
Fudge Pie 89

G

Garlic Brown-butter Chicken With Tomatoes 71
Garlic Lime Tahini Dressing 47
Glazed Duck With Cherry Sauce 70
Goat Cheese Bruschetta With Tomatoes 39
Green Curry Beef 57
Grilled Apple Fries With Caramel Cream Cheese Dip 83
Grilled Artichokes With Garlic Aioli 33
Grilled Banana S'mores 87
Grilled Carrots With Honey Glazed 47
Grilled Cornish Hens 66
Grilled Mozzarella And Tomatoes 26
Grilled Mozzarella Eggplant Stacks 25
Grilled Sausage Mix 14
Grilled Strawberry Pound Cake 84
Grilled Vegetable Quesadillas 36

H

Ham And Cheese Cups 11

Ham And Corn Muffins 16
Herbed Grilled Chicken Thighs 74
Homemade Bbq Chicken Pizza 39
Honey Rosemary Chicken 75
Honey-lime Glazed Grilled Fruit Salad 16
Honey-sriracha Brussels Sprouts 24
Honey-walnut Shrimp 78

I

Italian Baked Tofu 23

J

Jalapeño Poppers 44

K

Korean-style Steak Tips 56

L

Lamb Rack With Pistachio 56
Lemon And Rosemary Chicken 76
Lemon Dijon Vinaigrette 47
Lemon-garlic Butter Scallops 80
Lemony Chicken And Veggie Kebabs 66
Lime-garlic Grilled Chicken 71
Loaded Zucchini Boats 27

M

Maple Butter Corn Bread 38
Maple Walnut Pancake 13
Maple-teriyaki Chicken Wings 72
Mini Caprese Pizzas 17
Mixed Berry Dutch Baby Pancake 17
Mom's Lemon-pepper Salmon 79
Mozzarella Broccoli Calzones 31
Mozzarella Meatball Sandwiches With Basil 54
Mozzarella Sticks 44
Mushroom And Spinach Calzones 41
Mushroom And Squash Toast 20

N

Nut And Seed Muffins 8

O

One-pot Nachos 43
Orange And Honey Glazed Duck With Apples 72
Orange Cake 83
Orange-ginger Soy Salmon 77

P

Peaches-and-cake Skewers 88
Peanut Butter-chocolate Bread Pudding 90
Pear And Apple Crisp 82
Pecan-crusted Turkey Cutlets 65
Perfect Grilled Asparagus 27
Pesto Egg Croissantwiches 21
Pico De Gallo 48
Pork Chops In Bourbon 51
Pork Chops With Creamy Mushroom Sauce 63
Pork Sausage With Cauliflower Mash 49
Pork Spareribs With Peanut Sauce 48
Potato And Prosciutto Salad 50

Pulled Pork Sandwiches 54

R

Rack Of Lamb Chops With Rosemary 59
Roasted Chicken Tenders With Veggies 65
Roasted Lemony Broccoli 30
Rosemary And Garlic Lamb Pitas 53
Rosemary Roasted Potatoes 26
Rosemary Roasted Squash With Cheese 27
Rum Grilled Pineapple Sundaes 91

S

Salsa Verde Chicken Enchiladas 67
Sesame-thyme Whole Maitake Mushrooms 35
Shrimp Boil 78
Simple Corn Biscuits 81
Simple Pesto Gnocchi 33
Simple Whole Chicken Bake 75
Sizzling Pork Sisig 58
Smoky Paprika Pork And Vegetable Kabobs 64
Sourdough Croutons 18
Spaghetti Squash Lasagna 61
Spiced Breaded Chicken Cutlets 75
Spicy Beef Lettuce Wraps 52
Spicy Cauliflower Roast 24
Spicy Chicken Kebabs 74
Spicy Kale Chips 42
Spinach With Scrambled Eggs 10
Sriracha Golden Cauliflower 32
Steak And Lettuce Salad 63
Strawberry Pizza 85
Stuffed Bell Peppers With Italian Maple-glazed Sausage 15
Stuffed Spinach Chicken Breast 68
Swedish Beef Meatballs 62
Sweet And Tangy Beef 57
Sweet Chili Turkey Kebabs 67
Sweet Pepper Poppers 34
Sweet Potato Chips 40
Sweet Potato Fries With Honey-butter Sauce 46

T

Teriyaki Chicken And Bell Pepper Kebabs 69
Teriyaki Pork And Mushroom Rolls 58
Tomato And Lamb Stew 52
Tomato-corn Frittata With Avocado Dressing 11
Tomato-stuffed Grilled Sole 77
Turkey Meatballs With Cranberry Sauce 73

U

Ultimate Skillet Brownies 91
Uncle's Famous Tri-tip 62

V

Vegetable And Cheese Stuffed Tomatoes 35
Vegetarian Meatballs 34
Veggie Taco Pie 32
Vietnamese Pork Chops 53

Printed in Great Britain
by Amazon